THE EFFECTS OF
UNEMPLOYMENT IN IRELAND:

a report of a conference organised by
Co-operation North

Edited by Eithne McLaughlin

ISBN: 0 948297 07 7
Published by Co-operation North,
October 1993
Copyright: Co-operation North

Printed by

THE EFFECTS OF UNEMPLOYMENT IN IRELAND:

report of a conference organised by
Co-operation North,

Dundalk, 26th and 27th November 1992

Edited by Eithne McLaughlin

with the assistance of Carolyn Comer

ACKNOWLEDGEMENTS

Co-operation North would like to thank all those who contributed to the 1992 Conference on Unemployment, upon which this report is based. Co-operation North does not specialise in the field of unemployment and it would not have been possible for us to make this contribution to debate on such an important issue without the work of the Conference Steering Committee – Dr Eithne McLaughlin, Queen's University of Belfast; Chris Campbell, Belfast Centre for the Unemployed; Dr Andrew Finlay, Centre for Applied Health Research, University of Ulster; Mike Allen, Irish National Organisation of the Unemployed; Larry Bond, Combat Poverty, Dublin. Thanks also to Fr. MacGreil, Maynooth College, who served in an advisory capacity. The conference was attended by 76 people representing a wide range of people and organisations – they included policy-makers, service deliverers, researchers, trade unionists, the media, generalist community development and voluntary sector organisations and, of course, specialist groups and organisations of unemployed people. Special thanks must go to all those who agreed to make presentations. Last but not least, we would like to thank Cllr. Lucia Murray, Chair of the Dundalk Urban Council, who welcomed us to Dundalk, which, with an unemployment rate of 30%, was a most appropriate venue for the Conference.

Deirdre McKervey, Conference Organiser, Co-operation North.

CONTENTS

PART I: The Social and Health Effects of Unemployment

PART II: Responses to the Effects of Unemployment

FOREWORD

Tony Kennedy, Chief Executive, Co-operation North

Co-operation North aims to use practical co-operation across religious divides and territorial boundaries as a means to an end. The end being an increased tolerance and understanding of the traditions which share the island. At the same time as reassuring the Northern Irish people that their counterparts in the Republic of Ireland have no desire to dominate, we also encourage the people of the Republic of Ireland to realise that how they think, what they say and do, impact directly on what we have all come to know as the Northern Ireland situation.

Through such events as the 1992 conference on unemployment, people from both traditions in Northern Ireland have an opportunity to work together with their counterparts from the other side of the border on an issue of common concern. Through this process, greater appreciation of those aspects of life on this island which we share will emerge.

So why should an organisation whose primary function lies within the area of community relations be involved in supporting initiatives specifically on unemployment? There are a number of reasons for this. It is broadly recognised by most people in Northern Ireland that socio-economic as well as political and religious factors have contributed to 'The Troubles'. In order to fulfill Co-operation North's objectives therefore, work on issues of socio-economic significance allow people to share different approaches to common problems and allow networks to develop in order to create positive social change.

The issue of unemployment is an all-Ireland issue which has not only been discussed, but many millions of pounds on each side of the border have been spent in attempts to 'solve' the problem. Job creation strategies, while obviously important, have proven to have limits as the number of people out of work continues to grow. For this reason, Co-operation North are keen to ensure that while efforts are made to create jobs, alternative strategies dealing realistically with the needs of unemployed people, are also put in place.

When the issue of unemployment is debated, it is often the same organisations that are seen to comment and take action. In order that the maximum awareness and action on the matter is promoted, more voices must be heard. Through this publication and the conference upon which it was based, Co-operation North is lending its voice to the call for urgent action.

Many bridges have to be built in the course of Co-operation North's work. The intention of the all-Ireland Conference on the Social and Health Effects of Unemployment, organised and funded by Co-operation North, and held in Dundalk on 26th and 27th November 1992, was to build bridges between people who are unemployed and those who legislate or make policy for those who are unemployed. For real change there must be real understanding. Understanding of the needs of people who are unemployed and an understanding of the parameters within which policy makers operate. Some of the needs will have to be clarified and some of the parameters pushed back but without the bridge between needs and policy our work is misguided.

Co-operation North hopes that this report of the Dundalk conference will continue the Conference's contribution to this process. The report has been edited by Dr Eithne McLaughlin of the Dept. of Sociology and Social Policy at The Queen's University of Belfast, and is divided into two parts: first, examination of the nature and extent of the social and health effects of unemployment; and second, examples of statutory and community responses to these effects. The report is intended not as an academic document, but rather as a resource for those wishing to pick up on issues around unemployment, whether they be community groups, journalists, or policy-makers.

INTRODUCTION

Anna Lee, Manager, Tallaght PESP Partnership.

At the Dundalk Conference, it proved difficult to tie the discussion down solely to the health and social effects of unemployment. This is largely to do with the size and intractability of the problem. It is a huge problem that manifests itself in many ways and, in order to fully understand and tackle unemployment, an integrated and coherent approach is necessary.

What is important is not only the official rate of unemployment, but the attendant issues.

To quickly summarise the effects of unemployment, more fully discussed in the rest of this report:

unemployment = poverty = loss of opportunity = loss of choice = exclusion.

Discussion at the conference of the papers in this report centred around the following key points:

* The unemployed are often addressed as statistics, rather than as people.
* The unemployment figures are constantly being distorted.
* Too many employment and training schemes are in place in order to "massage" the unemployment figures and are not geared towards creating "real" jobs, paying decent wages.
* The larger political parties, North and South, are not interested in the voting power of the 20% or so of the working-age population who are unemployed.
* Unemployed people are not on the political agenda and therefore, have no voice.
* Unemployment is too often perceived as the fault of the unemployed.
* Unemployment is used as a threat to the workforce, which militates against any attempts to establish better conditions.

* It is not only those who have lost their jobs, who do, and should, worry about unemployment.
* Those who are made redundant tend to be unprepared for the impact upon their lives and this can lead to the destruction of whole communities and its esteem.
* Age militates against employment.
* It is important to face up to the fact that unemployment will continue to exist for the foreseeable future and stress-relieving measures, such as voluntary work and increased affordable leisure activities, need to be developed.

These are the strong messages which came across from discussion of some very powerful papers which are now included in this report. It is important to remember, however, that poverty and unemployment impact more extensively on some groups, such as women, people with disabilities, travellers, people who are long-term unemployed, or young people and older people too. Poverty and unemployment also have a greater effect on some communities than it does on others. They are not evenly distributed problems, but are located in communities that most of us can name and must also acknowledge.

The loss of self-worth and self-esteem consequent upon both unemployment and it's attendant poverty is the result of the fact that, although over 300,000 people in the Republic and 110,000 in the North are officially classified as unemployed (and many more do not even get as far as being officially recognised as unemployed), nevertheless, people are still defined in personal terms by their jobs. A major cultural and social shift is necessary to change this. People are still blaming themselves for their unemployment and their poverty because society forces these notions upon them. It is very true that unemployed people have no negotiating base, leaving them restricted and tied down.

In order to deal with these problems, the unemployed and the agencies who work on their behalf; the statutory agencies and government bodies; the legislators and policy-makers; and all those affected by unemployment and poverty must address the issue in an integrated way. Some of the efforts to date have yielded positive results – more have not. Without the necessary resources, however, this cannot be improved upon and once well-planned and worthwhile programmes are watered down to nothing. Schemes need to be altered, to reflect a real desire for jobs and this can better be achieved by consulting with those for whom the schemes are created.

The people who are affected by unemployment need to be heard and it is up to the policy-makers to provide the necessary platform. The unemployed and poor are not to be blamed for the problems of unemployment and poverty, rather society as a whole has a collective responsibility to urgently and effectively deal with the problem today. As this report shows, we are still far from such a position.

PART I:

THE SOCIAL AND HEALTH

EFFECTS OF UNEMPLOYMENT

1.1 Unemployment: The Politics of Contempt?

Eithne McLaughlin, Department of Sociology and Social Policy, The Queen's University of Belfast.

Introduction

What are the social effects of unemployment? The main effect is poverty which in turn creates layers of further effects:

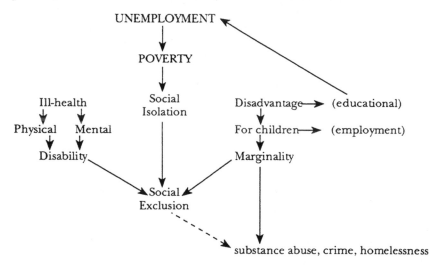

In the rest of this paper, I will try to outline how and when these phenomenon come about and are linked together. There is a need to lay out clearly the academic work on these issues because the 1980s/90s political climate – especially the rise of the New Right in Britain, the USA and to some extent in the Republic of Ireland – has led to a shift in the nature of public debate. The main dimension of this political climate has been that poverty is either said not to exist ("after all, we've got social security") or, if poverty is acknowledged to exist, the cause of it is attributed to the individual or group characteristics of poor people, rather than to unemployment, low pay, discrimination, etc.

The academic literature on unemployment

The academic economic and social policy literature on the consequences of unemployment is useful in so far as it is able to raise the level of public debate on these issues by providing some evidence, as opposed to anecdote, for or against political arguments on the causes and effects of unemployment. The first finding of that literature which I wish to emphasise is that unemployment causes a reduction in income levels (we can come onto whether this is the same as poverty later): studies have shown that only a very small minority of unemployed people are 'better off' on the dole that they would be in employment. If we compare income levels in and out of work, we find that being 'better off on the dole' could happen only occasionally. In both the Republic and Northern Ireland out-of-work benefit levels are so low that it is not hard for a job to provide a better overall income. For example, in Northern Ireland such a problem would be largely confined to two-parent families with 4 or more dependant children or to lone-parents with two or more very young children, and hence very high childcare costs, and/or to those faced with the prospect of not just low-paid jobs, but *very* low paying jobs (for example, full-time jobs paying £60/70 net a week). Further evidence of the gap in standard of living of people out of work compared to people in work is that unemployed people spend two-thirds as much of their incomes as those in work on food, and just over half as much on clothing (see the Family Expenditure Surveys in Britain).

Unemployment and marital breakdown are now the two biggest causes of low incomes – it is often thought that old age is the biggest cause but that is no longer true in Northern Ireland and Britain, where improvements in older people's incomes and declines in the relative incomes of families with children means that unemployment and lone parenthood are now more significant. Between 1979 and 1987 in Britain and Northern Ireland, the number of people on the lowest incomes due to unemployment more than tripled. In 1987, 42% of the poorest tenth of the population were unemployed. Families in the bottom tenth income group in Britain and Northern Ireland saw a 14% fall in their real income after housing costs between 1978 and 1990 (Households Below Average Income, 1993), compared with a 30% rise for the whole population. 40% of households in this bottom group were couples with children and 9% were lone-parents. There are two main reasons for this fall in real income for the poorest: a) reductions in income tax but not VAT and b) restraints on the levels of, and access to, social security benefits.

The level of social security benefits available to unemployed people with children and lone parents means that once people have been receiving them for, say six months to a year, day-to-day living becomes marked by:

- inadequate diet (in terms of nutrition and occasionally in terms of quantity) (with people having to make hard choices between eating and heating, or eating and shoes for the kids). The British Ministry of Agriculture has just attempted to produce a healthy weekly diet for people on social security and the results were dreadful – one egg every two weeks, dry bread (see Leather 1992 for further detail);
- reliance on second-hand clothes;
- insufficient furniture;
- inefficient heating systems (because no capital is available to install efficient systems   and good insulation);
- inability to participate in active forms of social life (eg days out to the zoo, museums, cinemas, bowling alleys, adventure playgrounds, visiting family where an-out-town journey is involved, pubs and clubs) and reliance on passive forms of social contact such as the TV;
- social isolation and monotony;
- fragile money management, where even relatively minor 'crises' (eg one of the family having to go into hospital, or the fridge breaking down) throws everything upside down;
- stress and anxiety.

These are usually summed up as 'it's existing, not living'. Many studies (for example, those by Bradshaw in Britain and by Evason in Northern Ireland) have shown that unemployed people do not have enough money to use public transport, have great difficulty buying shoes and clothes, and have inadequate stocks of clothes, and cut down on food. Three months into unemployment, two-thirds of young unemployed families in Britain can expect to be in debt (Heady and Smith 1989) – a situation which will worsen as the length of unemployment goes on.

Here it is important to note that long-term unemployment rose substantially in the 1980s in Northern Ireland and would have in the Republic of Ireland were it not for the effect of the Preretirement Allowance which took older unemployed workers off the unemployment register and reduced the proportion of long-term unemployed in the unemployment totals. In Britain and Ireland, each time there is a rise and fall in unemployment, the fall never quite goes back to the level there was before the rise began (a spiral pattern) and this 'sticky' nature of unemployment in Britain and Ireland throughout the 1970s and 1980s means that proportionately long-term unemployment has risen (Jackman 1992). It is the long-term unemployed for whom current levels of social security spell deprivation.

Social security policy in Britain and Northern Ireland has done nothing for long-term unemployed people over the last decade – in fact the reverse. There have been more than fifty changes to social security provision for unemployed people in the North. These have involved many more disqualifications from benefit, and cuts in the levels of benefits (in terms of purchasing power), and a worsening situation for unemployed people with children (who were already the worst off of the unemployed when the decade began).

I have said that current levels of social security benefits spell deprivation for the long-term unemployed but it might be useful to summarise here what the academic literature says about whether what I have called 'deprivation' constitutes 'poverty'. The majority academic view is that the levels of social security benefits in Britain and Northern Ireland and the Republic of Ireland, especially for people with children, result in people being unable to participate in the customary activities of their society or to fulfill what would be the normal obligations inherent in, and expectations of, common social roles – such as those of membership in an extended family, friendship, and even those of parenthood. This inability to participate more broadly means that many people living for long periods on social security are effectively denied full social and political citizenship or involvement in society. Together with the (related) evidence of the effect of poverty and unemployment on physical and mental health, this must constitute poverty.

The minority view is that this does not constitute poverty because social security does give people a minimum and allows them to continue to exist, if not live, and albeit with worse standards of health then the rest of the population (see Nolan and Whelan, section 1.3). Typical arguments in support of the 'this is not poverty' view, would include the fact that many unemployed people nowadays own consumer goods such as TVs, videos, fridges, washing machines, which they would not have done 20 years ago. And that most unemployed people manage to find money to spend on non-necessities like cigarettes and alcohol. Most such arguments fail to take into account the whys and wherefores of how people on social security spend their money.

As regards ownership of consumer durables, many unemployed people bought these when they were employed – the running costs of these items are low and it would make little sense to sell, say, a five year old TV for the £20-odd it would fetch. Other unemployed people procured these items while they were unemployed but bought them second hand at a very low cost. Equally, others own washing machines, fridges, etc. which do not work properly and ought to be replaced but which cannot afford to be. So survey statistics which show that, say, 75% of unemployed people own a washing machine, actually tell us virtually nothing about whether unemployed people are poor or not. The second issue of what unemployed people spend their money on is a debate overrun with a punitive morality – what are they doing spending £5 a week on cigarettes when they should be spending that on food for their kids? If only choices were that simple! To a harassed and depressed unemployed mother, it may be a case of spending £5 a week on cigarettes or strangling the children. It may be that the £2.50 a week spent on a few cans of beer consumed with family and friends in one of their homes, is actually a very cheap way of maintaining some social contact with others – and with the benefits to mental health that social contact provides, it's cheap at the price.

It is also true that there can be a lot of conflict about what money should be spent on between husbands and wives, and what the money ends up being spent on, will reflect who wins in those conflicts, and whose interests they have been promoting. When women are financially dependent on men as most mothers are in the Republic and North of Ireland, no assurances can be given about whether they are in poverty or not, whatever the income of the husband-father. If the household income is given to the man, as most social security benefits are, women and children may experience more intense poverty than he does, or they may be in poverty when he is not. Their fate depends on the individual man's approach to the household's income – if he thinks he should have a tenner for 'pocket money', then the likelihood is he'll have it; if he thinks that £30 a week is enough to buy and food and clothes for the whole house, then that's what she will have. This kind of poverty is never acknowledged by government – for example, the British government in it's 1985/86 review of the social security system simply said that, for unspecified reasons, governments "have to trust" the man to share out income equally. What a contemptuous response to the rights of women and children to adequate standards of nutrition, heating and clothing!

But of course this point – that how people spend their incomes is a complex matter – gets swept to one side by the emotional language with which poverty is discussed and debated in the media and parliamentary politics and it is to this language that I want to now turn.

The Language of Poverty and the 'Underclass'

From the 1600s onwards, successive governments in Britain and Ireland have divided poor people into the deserving and the undeserving, the respectable and the rogues. In other words, in terms of morals, not money. The deserving poor were those who unavoidably could not take paid employment and hence had little or no income – they were too old, or they had a substantial impairment or long severe illness, or were too young. The undeserving poor were those who would not take employment and hence had no real right to state protection. The significance of this dual moral categorisation of the poor has been phenomenal because it has shaped the nature and level of social security provision for unemployed people. It has not, however, served to protect the 'deserving poor' because the low levels of support for the undeserving have influenced and held down and support for sick people, disabled people, lone mothers, elderly people, and so on. The implications of this way of thinking about poverty are two-fold:

1. poverty caused by lack of employment can be reinterpreted as poverty caused by individual's own weak morals;
2. the alleviation of poverty among even the deserving must be held back, kept down, ungenerous, in order that the undeserving do not get access to state support that they do not deserve, by passing themselves off as deserving (such is the difficulty of judging other individual's morals that such 'passing' is presumed to be easy).

The introduction of the Beveridge welfare state in Britain after the Second World War took place in a haze of temporary political consensus, in which considerations of the deserving/undeserving distinction for once took second place to ideas of rights and social insurance, though they did not disappear. This back-seat did not last for long. A mere fifteen to twenty years later, in the 1960s, the deserving/undeserving wolf appeared in new clothing as the 'culture of poverty'. According to the 'culture of poverty', there was a substrata of families, and even whole communities, who were psychologically incapable of taking opportunities which were available to them and thus help themselves out of poverty (Lewis 1968). Politically the main advocate of this new wolf in sheep's clothing in Britain was Keith Joseph, who popularised the 'culture of poverty' as the 'cycle of deprivation'. No great insight is required to see the parallels between the deserving/undeserving way of seeing the poor and the concept of a 'cycle of deprivation'. Common to both is the assumption that poverty is significantly caused by the weak moral fibre of the poor.

Another 15-20 years on and we are again seeing these tired, hackneyed old terms revitalised and revived – this time by the use of the term underclass. What is meant by an underclass? In their revival, New Right writers and politicians are using a concept called 'behavioural poverty' to define 'underclass'. That is, a notion that poverty is the product of poor people's behaviour – which in turn is a result of their 'attitudes', the late 20th century version of morals. The underclass, apparently, do not subscribe to the morals of mainstream society – they do not value work, thrift, marriage, have little sense of personal obligation and none of obligation to society. As a result their lifestyle is dominated by instability, failure to look ahead to the future, for example, through saving, staying on in education, etc., and a lack of respect for others, demonstrated in lack of respect for the agencies of collective authority such as the police, social workers, etc. Their different moral values mean that they do not take up opportunities that are available, careering instead from one crisis to the next, causing their own poverty. This behavioural poverty, so New Right writers argue, is then contributed to, even caused, by social security benefits, which provide an easy option for living out these 'alternative' values.

Writers such as Charles Murray have successfully popularised this kind of usage of the term underclass and it is now used freely by the media. Lister (1990) has pointed out what a dangerous concept it is. It is impossible to prove whether an underclass in this sense exists or not because the term is so imprecise that it gets stretched to mean the poor generally, so that elderly pensioners get lumped in with young single drug-abusing black males. The term is not only imprecise, it is also disturbing – 'it is the language of disease and contamination' (Lister 1991). Murray, for example, in his Sunday Times article in 1989 described himself as 'a visitor from a plague area (the USA) come to see whether the disease is spreading'. Language such as this is value-laden and emotive, it contains a purely pathological view of people in poverty, implies that they are to be feared (and that perhaps society needs to be 'cleansed' of them), and sets poor people apart from the rest of society.

But these dimensions of the language of 'underclass' are politically very useful, allowing politicians to play on two of the most powerful of human emotions – fear and envy. Envy that anyone might escape what everyone at times has felt to be the onerous burden of social convention and fear of physical violence and theft. Not unexpectedly, the nature of underclass membership is different for men and women according to New Right writers. In the case of women, it is shown by having illegitimate children; in the case of men, the symptom is avoidance of employment:

> 'If illegitimate births are the leading indicator of an underclass and violent crime a proxy measure of its development, the definitive proof that an underclass has arrived is that large numbers of young healthy low-income males choose not to take jobs'. (Murray 1989).

This revival of the ages-old attribution of the causes of poverty to immorality and personal inadequacy was evident in the British Social Security Minister's speech to the Conservative Party Conference in 1992. He divided social security claimants into two – the genuine/decent and the not-genuine/indecent. The not-genuine were, on the female side, young single mothers and, on the male side, malingerers (the so-called sick who aren't really sick) and fraudsters (not really looking for work or already working).

Evidence of the 'undeserving poor'
What can academic literature contribute to an assessment of this 'behavioural poverty' thesis?

Firstly, there is no evidence that the existence of social security benefits for unemployed people, encourages other people to give up their jobs and become unemployed (see Dilnot 1992 for a review). Secondly, the only effect that can be found is that the availability of unemployment benefits makes the duration of unemployment on average marginally longer but the effect is very slight (Dilnot 1992). Third, there is little evidence of resignation, passivity, 'giving up' on employment, even among the very long-term unemployed who continue to apply for jobs even after hundreds of 'rejections' (McLaughlin et al 1989).

Therefore there is no evidence that large numbers of unemployed people avoid employment.

There is also no evidence that unemployed people sit around waiting for even a reasonably well-paid job to appear – they apply for jobs paying far less than average wages, far less than they themselves previously earned if they were employed before (Moylan et al 1984, McLaughlin et al 1989), and even apply for jobs in which their incomes in work would be about the same as their incomes out of work. The only pervasive constraint on their attitudes to possible employment is that if they have children, or are hoping to have them soon, employment must be able to provide for their 'basic needs' (Jordan et al 1992, McLaughlin et al 1989). As regards lone parenthood, young single women consciously deciding to get pregnant in order to get a council house or lone parents benefits, have not been found by any researchers. Some women on the other hand do become lone parents in order to escape severe hidden poverty within marriage (that is, hidden poverty contributes to marital breakdown rates). Finally, there is no evidence that poor people spend the meagre income they get in any more unwise ways than anyone else, nor that they generally aspire to some kind of 'alternative' lifestyle.

There is, then, a huge lack of evidence to support the Murray type of 'behavioural poverty' idea. What emerges instead from the most detailed academic work on unemployment is the overwhelming desire on the part of the majority of unemployed people to be part of 'mainstream' society. This is especially the case among those with children, or thinking about having children. There is no evidence that the majority of unemployed people are part of some kind of alternative, subversive sub-culture, with different values than those of people who happen to be employed. What is clear is that unemployed people themselves define poverty as being *forced* out of that mainstream society, as being unable to participate in the customary activities of society, because of lack of money.

Despite the lack of evidence to support the old deserving/ undeserving, or the newer 'culture of poverty'/underclass' thesis, these ideas have historically been the primary influence on the level of social security benefits. In order to preserve 'incentives' to take paid work, benefits had to provide the minimum necessary for existence or 'subsistence' as it was most often. This has resulted in a dis-spiriting search for the minimum calorie levels needed by different kinds of people, the minimum that is needed for household maintenance, the minimum margin of error that should be left for 'inefficient spending' (that is, people spending unwisely). The pseudo-scientific nature of this activity can all too easily lead us to overlook *why* so much anxiety and soul-searching is devoted to it (the essentially political belief that if you give people 'too much' when they are not employed, then they won't want to work). In the light of this, it is not surprising to find that the level of social security benefits in the North and South of Ireland has been such as to keep people in poverty rather than to take them out of it.

The effects of poverty
Having concluded that the Murray-type of underclass idea is without foundation, however, we are left with a couple of problems. Some British social scientists have argued that a small underclass is emerging (Giddens 1973; Hall 1987, Dahrendorf 1987) with one main characteristic – exclusion from the primary labour market. That is, that the same people are ending up in unemployment over and over again and when they are employed are in a secondary labour market of temporary, marginal jobs (Pissarides and Wadsworth 1992). Typically, the groups of people who are so affected are disabled people, working-class women, blacks, people in specific geographical areas (either inner-cities, or peripheral and rural regions), and in the North of Ireland, Catholics. The second problem is that if, on the one hand, we conclude that long-term unemployment has negative effects on people's mental health, leading to depression, demoralisation, withdrawal (Fryer 1992), and yet, on the other hand, we conclude that there is no 'culture of poverty' transmitted from generation to generation, how do we explain the apparent connection between poverty and street

violence, between poverty and crime, between poverty and drug abuse, between poverty and specific youth sub-cultures involving drug use and crime? If social scientists have found that the majority of unemployed people, especially if they have children, are remarkably similar to everyone else – they want to have the same things, to do the same things, hold the same values (Smith 1992), how then can one argue that governments need to act to reduce unemployment, because high levels of unemployment and the poverty that goes with it, are `a cause' of violence, of crime, of drug use, of early pregnancy, etc?. Yet in their representations to local and central government, those are precisely the reasons used to back up requests for funding work in areas of high unemployment.

Can we have it both ways, or are we obliged to subscribe to a pathological view of poor people in order to secure funding to improve their situation? I think we can 'have it both ways' though I think the problem is that we have not yet got to the point where we can express the connections between all these things very clearly. It is obvious that it is not being unemployed in itself which makes people become violent – other wise all unemployed people would be violent and they are not – yet drug abuse has something to do with unemployment, while growing up and living in a high unemployment area, in an inner-city ghetto or on an-out-of-town sprawling housing estate, are related to higher rates of street violence, substance-abuse and early pregnancy. It seems to me that the 'somethings' are to do with:

1. High rates of unemployment among both the young and adult populations in such areas, leading the younger generation to see that we are talking of a lifetime of unemployment for them.
2. High levels of exposure to a consumption-oriented society through the TV etc. – a symptom of the increasing gap between the haves and the have-nots, ie. the extent of inequality, which is different than the situation even 20 years ago when the haves didn't have so much.
3. What people learn about their worth (or lack of it) through watching their parents, older siblings, etc. face the daily humiliations of asking the milkman to hold on to next week, of borrowing a bucket of coal, of tense visits to the social security office of the housing office ... What one learns

through all this is that money gives you power and lack of money makes you a piece of rubbish in the eyes of those who have it. Of course, we learn about relationships between people in many ways, but one very important way is by seeing how money changes hands between people. What do these exchanges teach us about the worth of different things of people, what do these exchanges teach us about power – how to get it, what it means once you've got it, what it's like to be without it?

> "Poverty is not only about shortage of money. It is about rights and relationships; about how people are treated, and how they regard themselves; about powerlessness, exclusion and lack of dignity. Yet the lack of an adequate income is at its heart'. (Faith in the Church, 1985)

It is in such a contemporary context that social isolation for unemployed people and other poor people, could be becoming social exclusion, and that for some young people in particular the only sensible reaction is to ditch it all and develop a different life among people like yourself, one which is not dependant on self-worth derived from employment, having the right things in your home, even having a home, and/or to grab what you can of the affluence you are never going to have by fair means. This does fit with what we know of the relationship between crime and poverty – that it is driven by inequalities in consumption between the haves and the have-nots (a definitive review by Simon Field for the GB Home Office Research Unit in 1990 concluded that the key determinant of crime was not unemployment but consumption levels and inequalities). And it is true that in some areas of high unemployment, large changes in housing, courtship and family formation do seem to be taking place among 'excluded' young people (see, for example, White, 1991). In conclusion, there probably is a step beyond the social isolation, stress and anxiety which the majority of unemployed people have, and do, experience. And it may be a step which some younger unemployed people are *beginning* to take. For them social isolation may become an imposed social exclusion and permanent marginality, from which the only way out is a different set of social and political values – values hinging around the experience of each day as it comes, leaving them vulnerable to the temptations of the high-risk temporary highs which can be got from joyriding, drug abuse, unprotected sex, crime, gang warfare, etc. And so it is that unemployment now is *not* like unemployment in the 1920s and the 1930s -the social, economic and political context has changed, and it is that context that policy-makers and activists must address with a sense of realism and an absence of false moralising.

Concluding remarks

The academic study of poverty seems to many something of a contradiction in terms, and there has always been a danger that:

> '[the academic] discussion [of] poverty [may become a] debate worthy of Nero – a semantic and statistical squabble that is parasitic, voyeuristic and utterly unconstructive and which treats 'the poor' as passive objects for attention, whether benign or malevolent – a discussion that is part of the problem rather than part of the solution' (Piachaud 1987).

I hope, however, that this paper will have demonstrated some use-value in the large volume of research and writing on poverty which has been contributed by academic social scientists. any use-value, or solution-potential, this work may have is dependant on the messages it has being accessible to, on the one hand, people active in the voluntary and community sector, and on the other, people formally employed in policy-making and political circles – and that is the potential value of this contribution to debate facilitated by Co-operation North.

REFERENCES

Faith in the City, (1985), Report of the Archbishop of Canterbury's Commission on Urban Priority Areas, Church House.

Dahrendorf, R. (1987) 'The erosion of citizenship and its consequences for us all', in *New Statesman,* 12th June.

Dilnot, A. (1992) 'Social Security and the Labour Market' in McLaughlin, E. (ed) *Understanding Unemployment: new perspectives on active labour market policies,* Routledge.

Evason, E. (1987) *On the Edge,* CPAG, Derry.

Fryer, D. (1992) 'Psychological or Material Deprivation ?' in McLaughlin, E (ed) *Understanding Unemployment: new perspectives on active labour market policies,* Routledge.

Giddens, A. (1973) *The Class Structure of Advanced Societies,* Hutchinson.

Hall, S. (1987) 'Britain 2013' in *New Society,* 18 Dec.

Leather, S. (1992) *Your Food: whose choice?,* National Consumer Council, HMSO, London.

Lewis, O. (1968) *La Vida,* Penguin.

Lister, R. (1991) 'Concepts of Poverty' in *Local Government Policy Making,* February.

McLaughlin, E., Millar, J. and Cooke, K. (1989) *Work and Welfare Benefits,* Avebury.

Moylan, S., Millar, J. and Davies, R. (1984) *For Richer, for Poorer: DHSS cohort study of the unemployed,* DHSS/HMSO, London.

Murray, C. (1989) 'Underclass' in *The Sunday Times Magazine,* 26th November.

Murray, C. (1990) *The Emerging British Underclass,* IEA Health and Welfare Unit.

Piachaud, D. (1987) 'Problems in the definition and measurement of poverty' in *Journal of Social Policy,* 16,2.

Pissarides, C. and Wadsworth, J. (1992) 'Unemployment Risks' in McLaughlin, E. (ed) *Understanding Unemployment: new perspectives on active labour market policies,* Routledge.

Smith, D. (ed.) (1992) *Understanding the Underclass,* PSI, London.

White, M. (1991) *Against Unemployment,* PSI, London.

1.2   Unemployment – extent and effects

Brendan Mackin, Belfast Centre for the Unemployed.

Figures just released (Sept. 1992) by the Central Statistical Office show the recession maintaining its grip, following nine quarters of flat and falling output. The C.S.O. statistics coincided with a Bank of England report which showed that companies are shedding labour at an accelerating rate. Evidence of this include the announcements of the loss of another 10,000 jobs by British Rail, Blue Circle, Bank of Scotland, Eagle Star – more locally, Shorts in Belfast shed 1,000 jobs last year. Unemployment has reached its highest level for five-and-a-half years. In the UK it is 2.9 million, in the Republic of Ireland, over 300,000, and in Northern Ireland, it is 110,000. Stark though these figures may be, many people, including myself, believe them to be a grievous underestimation of the reality.

Since 1979, there has been 30 government changes to the method of calculation of the unemployed in the UK. In 1989, research by Coopers & Lybrand, exposed that the changes had removed 34,000 from the Northern Ireland count. A recent analysis by the Unemployment Unit in London shows the underestimate in the U.K. of 1.2 million, giving a total of 4 million unemployed. In addition, government statistics on unemployment count only the unemployed person him or her-self, and thus ignore the wider reality of its effect on families, dependents, and communities. And I believe the wider perspective must be considered if the real cost of unemployment is to become evident.

Taken in the wider context of unemployment, the Belfast Centre for the Unemployed has consistently questioned the motives behind the Government decision to manipulate unemployment statistics. The only conclusion we can reach is that there is a deliberate political policy to hide the unemployed. Moreover, this has been complemented with the shifting responsibility for unemployment from the Government to the individual. However, although by changing the definitions of 'unemployment', governments can hide information on the extent of unemployment, governments cannot hide the effects.

To put it bluntly, it is my belief that there are statistics and there is reality – and the reality is quite simple. Unless we understand the problem, any problem and the extent of that problem, then a solution will not be found.

Hiding the unemployed will not forever hide the lack of policy needed to address the problem. Neither will unemployment be solved by shifting the blame for unemployment to the individual. Throughout the 1980's the poor were confronted by a government which was largely indifferent to their plight. Those who raised the issue of poverty were publicly accused by Mrs Thatcher of "drooling and drivelling". This was followed by the then Secretary of State for Social Security, John Moore, who in a widely reported speech asserted that "there was no such thing as poverty in modern Britain".

This attitude has had a significant impact on social policy, which is clearly demonstrated in the reduction of welfare benefits, and the attacks on the social support mechanisms of the health service, public housing, education, local government services, all of which the unemployed and others in poverty are most dependent upon.

Unemployment has always been a major cause of poverty among those who were unskilled or semi-skilled, single parents, women, etc. . . But more recently redundancy is affecting those who previously thought they were in secure employment. Unemployment is now a reality for skilled and managerial grades in both the public and private sectors. Culturally, unemployment is a shock for these individuals and their families, with the loss of income and self esteem, which is then followed by the practical problems of having to cope with substantial and unserviceable debt, for example, mortgages, cars etc,. Their plight is exacerbated by the value of assets in a depressed market which cannot be realised. The growth and re-composition of the unemployed has helped to put unemployment and poverty back on the political agenda. The "new unemployed" are articulate and voters. Paradoxically the long term unemployed tend not to vote – approximately only 40% in the last general election in the UK and substantially lower in local elections.

The link between unemployment and poverty is now evident. Britain in common with Germany, uses social security benefits as both the definition of poverty and the means to tackle it. As I have already stated, the denial by Mrs Thatcher and her ministers that poverty exists, was followed by a severe reduction in the level of benefits.

A recent report by the Child Poverty Action Group (*The Wrong Side of the Tracks*) shows that the value of the Dole has fallen by nearly 40% in real terms. The report warns that unemployment and poverty are inexorably linked and warns that any further cuts in benefit will only deepen an already worsening situation. The report shows that Unemployment Benefit for a married couple with two children aged 5-10 years was £42.67 in 1979. Today, that same couple would receive £69.70. Using 1979 as a relative value of 100%, the present level is only 66%.

Needless to say Unemployment Benefit is not the only benefit which has been cut. The link between state pensions and earnings has been broken, young people are disbarred from benefits, grants under supplementary benefit have been abolished and replaced social fund loans under income support, child benefit has been frozen for many years, and means-testing is now the norm. All of these have combined to deepen poverty, and, except for pensions, the rest bear particularly heavily on the unemployed.

The long-term unemployed receive means-tested income support rather than Unemployment Benefit, and income support is at a lower level than Unemployment Benefit. A recent study, following a two year investigation by the Family Budget Unit, found that the living standards of families on income support are below the most basic level. Using a "low cost budget", based on what two thirds of the population judged to be necessities, the study found that an unemployed couple with two children get £105 per week while their costs would be £140 per week for the most meagre goods and services. The report concluded that families 'made up' the difference between income support and their needs by not replacing clothes, shoes and the adults, particularly the mother, going short on food.

To revert to statistics, the Low Pay Unit estimate that if we count the low paid and those on benefits, 12 million adults in Britain had incomes below the poverty line as defined by the European Council of Ministers.

Behind all the statistics and the levels of welfare benefits, what is the reality? What is it like for four people to live on £105 per week, that is, £3.75 each per day? Put more starkly, the price of two pints or a Big Mac, chips and coffee. But it is not only food, it is heat, light, clothes, shoes. In other words £20 for a pair of shoes leaves someone with only £6.25 to live on for a week. To do this financial balancing act for a week, a month, is difficult enough, but imagine what it is like year in, year out.

What are the financial dilemmas for parents with sick children? What is the impact of having to purchase school clothes? What is the cost of educational encouragement? How does deprivation affect childrens behaviour? What are the pressures on a marriage? Relate have found a yearly increase since 1989 of 15% in the numbers coming for counselling with the largest numbers of problems related to unemployment, that is, debts, domestic violence.

A new report by the Northern Ireland Voluntary Trust (*A Qualitative Study of Life in Disadvantaged Areas of Belfast*) gives a realistic insight into the lives of those on the poverty line. The report quotes people and their perspectives on poverty, employment opportunities, effects of unemployment, training schemes, obstacles, and general perceptions. To quote directly from the report on unemployed people's perceptions:

Poverty and Debt:

"You're so dependent. If you don't borrow you miss someone out – the milkman or the coalman or the electric. You live from day to day really. What people worry about is food on the table basically."

"I worry most about clothes and shoes for the kids. You can't even get a grant for uniforms for primary school. They say we can't give you this as the uniforms are not compulsory but any time my daughter is without a uniform she is pulled up about it. I went to the principal and asked for a letter saying the uniform was compulsory. She told me it wasn't but my daughter is still coming home saying, " I was shouted at today for no uniform".

"People go to money lenders. You've no choice but to go in the end if you need things for the house. What can you do? It's loans to pay loans.

"In this area I see them everyday – the tick men. There must be bongo drums or something because when they come down the street, one minute everyone is at their front door, the next minute everyone is away. There are still places where they take the family allowance books. It still goes on to this day".

"The real issue these days is poverty. Nobody actually wants to do anything about it. Most agencies want to ignore it. The contrast when you walk out of the middle of Belfast and go into some of the poorer areas is just enormous and it's getting worse and worse. But it's not the government's policy to get involved in that. It's policy is to have more shopping centres and that kind of thing. The issue now is that poverty isn't an issue."

Stress:

"A lot of women feel guilty about the fact that there isn't enough money coming in. It's always – you, you, you. I just sit and cry"

"It's always an underlying stress though in a family when there's a lot of unemployment because there are a lot of arguments."

Education – The Impact:

"My daughter passed the eleven plus and I could not send her to St. Dominics [Grammar]. I couldn't afford it. Plus, I am a single parent and there'd be the stigma and pressure because I couldn't afford the things they require".

"What really gets up my nose is we have all these ones to get women back into education. I got my O'levels. Last year I got a place on a degree. The letter came, they wanted #1,000 odd and I had six pence in my purse. I applied everywhere. It's a con with the women's groups – all they give is, wee days here and there, and high hopes, but if you're on a low income you're stuck".

Benefits – The Impact:

"It has got worse because the government has switched things around in a lot of ways. Instead of giving people the grants they're giving out loans. It's near enough impossible to get a grant now. You just have to borrow the money and then go into debt and struggle. You cut down on food and luxuries. I find people have to go without."

"Anybody on social security is on the poverty line already. To give them a loan and expect them to pay it back is stupid. The whole idea of the loans system in the first place is stupid."

"I got a crisis loan a couple of weeks ago – they took £21 off me a week to pay it back".

The Young Unemployed:

"Government assumes young people are dependent on their parents until they're 25 which is ridiculous. To get benefit 16-17 year olds have to fit certain criteria and that's not always accepted. They don't understand the situation those kids are coming from. It's creating a hidden homelessness problem because the kids are moving around from A to B."

Job Opportunities:

"If you went down to the dole office and said you wanted a job at £140 you've a good chance of getting your dole stopped. There's no chance of getting a job at £140."

"My brother works 72 hours a week for £93. He's in security. I work 30 hours for £83.".

"There's no such thing as job security today. Even the dole isn't secure these days".

"When they are starting anyone now they only start them as temporaries. When their two years are up they are paying them off – so it's like another ACE scheme. The Executive is doing it, the Council is doing it".

Benefits a Disincentive?

"Get us jobs and we'll see who wants to work."

"There's no happiness in people now. When De Lorean opened it was great for the people. It's not that people don't want to work, they were interested in learning skills."

Aspects of Unemployment:

"It's lack of money, nothing to do. You're continually depressed."

"It's day by day – till you die. You just go out and try and get something everyday – different jobs, some kind of money or scheme or whatever. You see your father and brother not getting any work and you know something is wrong. Then you go out and you can't get it and you think of your children coming behind you – what's going to happen to them? It's just going to be the same."

Looking for Work:

"In the Job Club you get fed up writing away to places and getting no reply. A man needs a job for his ego. A man who can't feel he can support his family can be very depressed. It's very stressful. You have to feel useful to somebody."

"The only way to get a job around here is word of mouth – who you know. If your brother, uncle or father worked in a place you would get in. It's nothing to do with advertising and the job markets".

Consequences of Unemployment:

"You get your dole money of say £60 for the fortnight and maybe go into town. You see a pair of jeans sitting in the shop, you just go in and steal them. I'd rather take the chance than pay £28 for a pair of jeans. You're not gonna give half of your brue away."

"If you have work, you have pride. You live more openly. You can plan to go on holiday and give Johnny a new pair of trousers. In an area of high unemployment people go down the chute. They start looking dirty and shabby and there's theft and crime."

"If the wife nags on the husband, the men feel inadequate because they can't provide for their families . . . then the marriage just breaks down, there is very high separation rate in . . . a lot of one parent families."

Training Schemes:

"Training, I spent two years training, what's the guarantee after that you are going to get a job? None – it all boiled down to keeping the unemployment figures down."

"These schemes are a road to no town – waste of time. What the kids need is permanent employment – something to aim for, work for decent jobs and prospects. ACE and YTP were always designed to cut the unemployment figures."

Low Benefits – Low Wages:

"I am doing thirty-one hours a week up there and getting £84, coming home with £70. All I am making out of this job is a fiver but it's a job and it stops you from going crazy."

"You haven't enough to buy kids clothes. That's why people are doing the double. I am cleaning, morning to night, £38 every fortnight."

"Why are people doing the double? Can you live on £85 a week – me and two kids.

"They're going after people who are doing the double to exist. People in business are getting done for fraud for £5 million and getting fined £2 million. People aren't doing the double for fraud – they're doing it to exist."

"When you talk about doing the double you think about the unemployed – they're the focus of attention but it means less of a problem for the employer. He doesn't have to put people through the books and if he wants he can get rid of them. They don't have any rights."

Concluding Remarks

These quotes only reinforce what we hear in the Unemployed Centre on a daily basis. Unemployment and poverty cannot only be measured in financial terms. It must also be measured on the overall effect, that is, the family, community, society and the individual. There is no need for the direction policy has taken in the 1980s. The link between benefits and disincentives to employment has not been proven. Research carried out by David Piachaud of the London School of Economics, found that five out of six unemployed people would prefer to work even if benefits were high. The work ethic is alive and well in Northern Ireland. Recent openings in Belfast by Marks & Spencers have attracted thousands of applicants for 200 part-time jobs. The Fire Service, Montupet, Shorts, have all experienced a similar response. The unemployed do not need reduced benefits as an incentive to work. Neither do they need the abolition of wage councils to create more opportunities. At the moment there are approximately 40 unemployed people for each advertised job vacancy. What is needed are jobs to be competed for, and quality training schemes linked to the demands of the economy. Most of all what we need is a political and economic policy which deals with the conditions which create unemployment, and not a policy for the unemployed. I would like to end by reminding people of the words of William Beveridge, founder of the post-war welfare state, words which are as relevant now as they were then:

"The main principles which should govern national finance in the future are few and simple. The first rule is that outlay in total, private and public, must always be enough for full employment. The second rule is that outlay, public and private should be directed by social priorities, putting first things first, the prevention of Want, Disease, Squalor and Ignorance before inessentials. Bread and health for all before cake and circuses for anyone. To submit to unemployment or slums or want, to let children go hungry or sick and old untended for fear of increasing the national internal debt is to lose all sense of proportion."
(From: *Full Employment in a Free Society*, 1942).

1.3   Unemployment and Health

Brian Nolan and Christopher T. Whelan,
The Economic and Social Research Institute, Dublin.

Introduction

Our objective is to set out briefly what is known about the relationship between unemployment and ill-health. We use evidence for Ireland where possible, but also draw on research carried out in Britain, the USA and elsewhere.

A number of points need to be made at the outset. The first is that if we see that people who experience unemployment have more ill-health than others, this does not necessarily mean that unemployment itself causes this ill-health. Obviously, it could work the other way around: illness could itself be contributing to the difficulties someone is having in the labour market. Serious or frequent illness could make it difficult for an individual to get a good education or to get and keep a "good" job. In addition to looking at the association between unemployment and ill-health, then, we are also interested in the causal processes at work, and it may not be easy to tease out the direction of the effects.

Secondly, it is important not to focus too narrowly on the relationship between being unemployed and being ill, without looking at the background structural factors which mean that both unemployment and ill-health are more likely to be experienced by certain types of people, from particular socio-economic backgrounds or environments. We will therefore also say something about the broad relationship between health and social class, to provide this context.

Thirdly, it is helpful to distinguish between physical and psychological ill-health: although they may interact with each other, it appears that there may be important differences between the two in the nature of the relationship with unemployment. We will talk first about physical health then, before turning to unemployment and psychological health.

Physical Ill-Health

The Black Report published in 1980 put health inequalities "on the map" in Britain, and has been influential in winning wider attention for the issue in other countries. It documented the fact that there were large differentials in both mortality and morbidity favouring the higher social classes, and that these had persisted over time despite improvements in health and social services. The most striking evidence related to premature mortality: around 1971 the death rate for men aged between 15-64 was almost twice as high for those in the bottom (unskilled manual) class as in the top (professional and managerial) one. Subsequent British data suggest that these differentials if anything widened rather than narrowed up to 1981. The basis for these findings is the comparison of information from death certificates, which include occupation, with Census data on the total numbers in each occupational group or social class.

Some recent research for the Republic of Ireland (Nolan 1990) using the same type of approach and methods has shown similar substantial differentials across socio-economic groups. Table 1 shows that, for men aged 15-64, the (standardised) mortality rate in 1981 was more than twice as great for the unskilled manual group as for the professional/managerial ones. The group for whom occupation is "unknown" had an even higher mortality rate than the unskilled manual one. Information on occupation is particularly likely to be missing from those who were unemployed for a considerable period, while unskilled manual workers experienced much more unemployment than the other identified groups. Lower socio-economic status is therefore associated with both more unemployment experience and considerably higher mortality rates than for other groups.

Again, the causation could run from health to unemployment and socio-economic status rather than vice versa, with ill-health leading individuals with a high risk of dying to move down or remain towards the bottom of the socio-economic hierarchy. This is not something one could prove or disprove by looking at data of this type. However, recent research using a British longitudinal database which has information for the same individuals for 1971 and 1981 has shown that health-related social mobility of this kind does not account for the observed mortality differentials between the classes (Fox, Goldblatt and Jones 1986).

Table 1: Mortality Rates for Men Aged 15-64 by Socio-economic Group, Rep. of Ireland, 1981.

Socio-economic Group	15-24	25-34	35-44	45-54	55-64	Standardised Mortality Rate
			death rate per 1,000			
Farmers	0.9	0.8	1.4	5.6	14.8	79
Farm labourers	1.6	1.3	3.1	4.6	15.2	86
Higher professional	0.2	0.3	0.8	3.5	12.8	55
Lower professional	1.5	0.5	1.4	5.5	16.0	79
Employers and managers	0.9	0.5	1.2	4.5	11.6	62
Salaried employees	1.0	0.6	1.5	3.6	15.2	71
Non-manual white collar	1.0	1.1	2.4	7.8	20.2	105
Non-manual other	1.8	1.2	2.0	6.2	20.1	104
Skilled manual	0.9	0.7	1.9	6.2	18.7	91
Semi-skilled manual	1.7	1.1	3.0	7.2	22.1	117
Unskilled manual	1.9	1.5	3.4	10.7	31.6	163
Unknown	3.0	6.8	6.8	13.4	25.9	174

The same British data also allowed researchers to focus specifically on the mortality between 1971 and 1981 of men who were unemployed in 1971. This showed that mortality among this group was even higher than would be expected on the basis of their social class composition. Unemployment at the starting-date was itself associated with "excess" mortality even given broader social class effects (Moser, Fox and Jones 1986). Again, this did not seem to be explained by selection effects.

We now turn from mortality to morbidity. The Black report had little data on morbidity, but since then a good deal of information on differentials across social classes in Britain has become available from general household surveys and special health and lifestyles surveys. For example, the annual General Household Survey shows about 25% of professional men aged 16-64 reporting a long-standing illness, compared with about 40% of unskilled manual men.

Similar information on self-reported long-standing illness was obtained for the Republic in the household survey carried out by the ESRI in 1987. As Table 2 shows, the percentage of adults reporting such illness was at least twice as high for the unskilled manual as for the professional and managerial classes (Nolan 1992). Evidence from studies which also obtained clinical data on respondents suggests a high degree of agreement with such self-reports.

Table 2: Chronic Physical Illness by Age and Social Class, Rep. of Ireland, 1987

Age Range	Social Class					
	higher profes- sional	lower profes- sional	other non- manual	skilled manual	semi- skilled manual	unskilled manual
	% reporting chronic illness					
15-34	5.1	2.9	5.3	9.2	7.9	10.0
35-44	5.6	5.8	9.4	11.2	15.4	12.3
45-54	11.0	13.0	16.7	19.2	23.5	27.0
55-64	23.5	22.0	28.2	28.9	32.6	44.7
65 and over	21.8	33.6	30.8	37.6	36.3	33.4
All	10.5	10.5	13.9	17.0	19.0	24.6

Many of those with serious long-standing illnesses will give their current labour force status as ill or disabled rather than unemployed, so the relationship with current unemployment is problematic. Nonetheless, those who are currently unemployed in the ESRI sample were more likely to report a long-standing illness than those in work, controlling for age. (For example, for those aged between 35 and 44, 16% of those currently unemployed but only 5% of employees reported such an illness). It is more the relationship between unemployment and ill-health over time which is the nub of the issue, though. The ESRI survey also reveals that those who had experienced unemployment in their careers were more likely to have also spent time away from work because of illness than those who had not experienced unemployment. Similarly, a high proportion of those who were away from work due to illness or disability at the time of the survey had also experienced unemployment during their careers.

The factors producing the observed relationship between physical ill-health and socio-economic background, and between ill-health and unemployment in particular, are complex and difficult to disentangle. The poverty and deprivation often associated with membership of lower socio-economic groups can have direct effects through, for example, poor nutrition and housing conditions, behavioural factors which may increase risk of particular illnesses are also more prevalent in lower socio-economic groups, and certain occupations may involve exposure to specific risks. As far as unemployment is concerned, it is suggested that the psychological stresses involved may also play an important role in increasing vulnerability to physical illnesses.

It is extremely difficult, with the types of data usually available, to distinguish the role of different factors, or to isolate the impact of unemployment per se from that of the broader socio-economic background from which those experiencing unemployment generally come.

Unemployment and Psychological Distress
A variety of studies employing rather different methodological approaches converge in establishing the causal impact of unemployment on psychological distress. In the ESRI survey conducted in 1987, the measure of psychological distress employed was the General Health Questionnaire (GHQ) in its 12-item format. The GHQ was designed by Goldberg (1972) among 3,000 households, as a screening test for detecting minor psychiatric disorders in the community. The items included in the measure are designed to give information about the respondent's current mental state. It is neither a measure of long-standing attributes of personality, nor an assessment of the likelihood of falling ill in the near future (Goldberg, 1972). It is most definitely not, however, a mere complaints inventory. It consists only of items that have been chosen from a substantial battery of items shown to discriminate between groups of respondents in terms of their likelihood of being assessed as non-psychotic psychiatric cases.

If the results of a set of GHQ scores are compared with an independent psychiatric assessment, the possibility of being a psychiatric case exceeds one half. In the case of the twelve-item version, the threshold score is two and all respondents scoring above this level will be classified as suffering from psychological distress. Since the conclusions we wish to draw remain true irrespective of whether a dichotomous or continuous measure is employed, we will present our results in terms of the former, not just because of their intrinsic interest but also because it facilitates the communication of our most important results.

Using the GHQ measure we find that, as can be seen from Figure 1, just over one in three of the unemployed come above the psychological distress threshold compared to one in fourteen of employees. The differentials between these groups on selected individual items are documented in Figure 2. Only departures from usual functioning are scored as pathological and not responses such as "no more than usual". Despite this, almost 36% of unemployed men give a response in the pathological category to the question regarding feeling unhappy and depressed. Over 20% or more in each case indicate that they have:

1. felt they could not overcome their difficulties;
2. lost much sleep over worry;
3. felt constantly under strain;
4. been losing confidence in themselves.

Figure 1

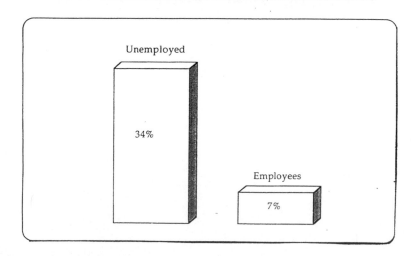

PERCENTAGE WITH SCORES ABOVE THE GENERAL HEALTH
QUESTIONNAIRE THRESHOLD: A COMPARISON OF
UNEMPLOYED AND EMPLOYEES

Unemployed

34%

Employees

7%

The disparities between the unemployed and the employees on such items range from two to one, to four to one. On perhaps the most extreme negative item in the set – "thinking of yourself as a worthless person" – the level of pathological response is lower for the unemployed than on the other negative items, that is, 14%. The differential, however, between the unemployed and employees of 17 to one is the highest on any of the items.

Figure 2

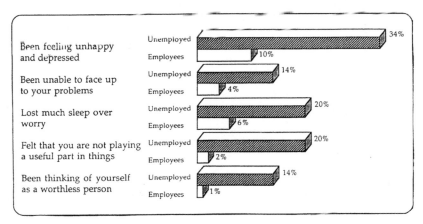

A COMPARISON OF THE LEVEL OF NEGATIVE RESPONSE
ON SELECTED GENERAL HEALTH QUESTIONNAIRE ITEMS
FOR UNEMPLOYED AND EMPLOYEES

Been feeling unhappy and depressed	Unemployed	34%
	Employees	10%
Been unable to face up to your problems	Unemployed	14%
	Employees	4%
Lost much sleep over worry	Unemployed	20%
	Employees	6%
Felt that you are not playing a useful part in things	Unemployed	20%
	Employees	2%
Been thinking of yourself as a worthless person	Unemployed	14%
	Employees	1%

Length of Unemployment

The concept of stages of unemployment which emerged in the literature of the 1930's has become a basic concept in accounts of the psychological effects of unemployment. Eisenberg and Lazarfield (1938: 378) concluded:

> "We find that all writers who have described the course of unemployment seem to agree on the following points: first there is shock, which is followed by an active hunt for a job, during which the individual is still optimistic and unresigned; he still maintains an unbroken attitude. Second, when all efforts fail, the individual becomes pessimistic, anxious and suffers active distress: this is the most crucial state of all. And third the individual becomes fatalistic and adapts himself to his new state but with a narrower scope. He now has a broken attitude."

Studies relating length of unemployment to mental health, however, have been far from consistent. Jackson and Warr (1984) suggest that the failure of early studies to find a relationship may have been due to the fact that the age range of respondents or the length of unemployment studied were too restricted. More recent studies suggest that the newly unemployed experience a deterioration in psychological health within weeks and that by three months this has become worse, but it then remains stable for long periods and might even improve (Fryer and Payne 1986).

Our own results, which are set out in Figure 3, show little difference between those unemployed for less than a year and those unemployed more than one year. These results are consistent with the finding in the literature. However, this contrast conceals some interesting differences. If we exclude those seeking their first job and those on State training schemes, we did find that levels of mental health decline beyond the second year of unemployment with the level of psychological distress increasing from 37% above the threshold for those unemployed for less than two years to 43% for those between two or three years, and to 54% for those above between three to four years. At this point, with the exception of this final result, our findings are consistent with the hypothesis of a gradual decline in psychological well being.

Figure 3

PERCENTAGE ABOVE GENERAL HEALTH QUESTIONNAIRE THRESHOLD SCORE BY LENGTH OF UNEMPLOYMENT

Percentage above GHQ Threshold

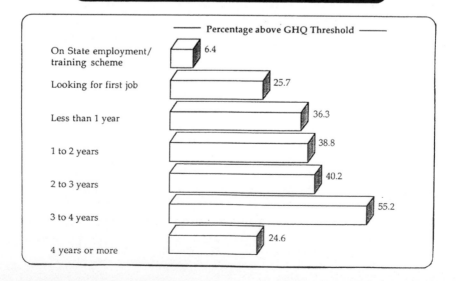

Length of unemployment	Percentage above GHQ Threshold
On State employment/training scheme	6.4
Looking for first job	25.7
Less than 1 year	36.3
1 to 2 years	38.8
2 to 3 years	40.2
3 to 4 years	55.2
4 years or more	24.6

The explanation of this latter finding requires that we turn our attention to the relationship between unemployment and poverty. It is important to keep in mind, as Kelvin and Jarrett (1985: 26) stress, that:

> "The description of stages does not itself provide an explanation of the effects of unemployment: at most it merely provides the first step towards it, and then only if the description is sufficiently accurate."

What is necessary, they argue, is to isolate the factors which determine the transition between stages and developments within them. Despite the attention devoted to stages, Kelvin and Jarrett (1985: 19-39) note that there have been very few attempts to trace the interaction of the economic and psychological effects of unemployment and to move beyond description and examine the systematic relationship between increasing poverty and changing reactions to unemployment.

Again, if we exclude those seeking their first job and those on State schemes, we find that the percentage falling below our line rises steadily with length of unemployment. This result makes our previous finding regarding the relatively low level of distress displayed by those unemployed for more than four years even more perplexing. This finding tends to undermine an explanation of the 'deviant' result in terms of participation in the "black economy". An alternative explanation could be offered in terms of coping adjustments. Warr and Jackson identify two particularly important mechanisms of adaptation to a new role and reduced commitment to finding a new job. This interpretation takes into account the fact that the initial period of unemployment may be particularly traumatic time. Gradually adaptation may take place. Daily and weekly routines become established, expenditure limits become clarified and behaviour may be shaped to avoid threats from new situations or other people (Warr and Jackson 1985: 805). A further adjustment arises form the calculation that the probability of obtaining paid work is low, with a consequent reduction in employment commitment and job seeking.

Set against such possibilities is the increased probability of poverty. It seems doubtful to us, in view of the latter, that such coping strategies could account for the results we have observed. It is necessary, therefore, to consider a further possibility raised by

Warr and Jackson (1985: 806) that the type of response alternative employed in our measure of psychological distress may lead to an underestimation of levels of distress of those in long-term unemployment. The GHQ may miss chronic disorders because it asks respondents for an assessment of symptoms in terms of categories such as 'same as usual'. This seems to occur less than might be expected on theoretical grounds because people cling rather stubbornly to the concept of their 'usual self'. It seems plausible, though that those unemployed for more than five years may have great difficulty in preserving such a concept.

It is necessary to emphasise, though, that although length of unemployment does produce some interesting effects, the differences are relatively modest. Such differences are much less important than the fact of being unemployed (Fryer and Payne 1986: 253). Similarly, previous unemployment has a weak effect. Thus, a mere two per cent more of those who had been unemployed in the past twelve months were above the GHQ case threshold than those who were at work and had never been unemployed. In relation to the impact of unemployment on physical health, the available evidence suggests that one should avoid an undue emphasis on current spell of unemployment since it diverts attention away from the accumulation of disadvantages over time. With mental health, on the other hand, it does appear that the current employment situation is critical. This finding is consistent with the evidence that re-employment leads very rapidly to dramatic improvements in mental health.

Unemployment, Poverty and Psychological Distress
In surveying the current literature on psychological distress, a compelling case can be made that its most striking feature is the remarkable lack of emphasis on poverty (see Fryer 1992 for a review). A great deal of the literature relating to the impact of unemployment on mental health has operated from a perspective that views levels of distress as influenced by life events, with unemployment constituting one such crucial life event.

The earlier studies espoused the idea that a straightforward numerical accumulation of experienced life events predisposes to illness. Underlying this approach is the assumption that events lead to stress because the organism is fundamentally intolerant of change, an assumption which was rooted in the pioneering laboratory studies. The natural state of the organism was seen as one of equilibrium.

Social scientists have increasingly questioned the notion that change per se is damaging. They have moved beyond notions relating to the number of events and the magnitude of change in terms of degree of adjustment and have focused attention on issues relating to the quality of events – desirability, degree of control, whether or not they are scheduled or unscheduled.

Unemployment is clearly an event which is predominantly undesirable, uncontrolled and unscheduled. It has generally been labelled an acute stressor and fits readily within the stressful life change approach. Stress, however, can follow both from change in the environment and lack of change (Wheaton 1980). It is useful to distinguish between acute stressors and chronic stressors. Chronic stress arises from the dogged, slow-to-change, problems of daily life, when pressures from the environment exceed the coping capacity of the person. The two types of stress converge when life changes have an impact by increasing the number and level of day-to-day life strains. The impact on emotional well-being in such cases arises, not from change itself, but from change that leads to hardship in basic enduring economic and social circumstances.

The most striking example of this process is when the crucial link between poverty and unemployment leads to economic hardship and social isolation both for individuals and their family. Kelvin and Jarrett (1985: 18) note that while those concerned with the psychology of work have long stressed that work provides much more than merely money, those concerned with unemployment need to stress that to be unemployed is frequently to be poor.

When we look at the relationship between poverty and mental health in the Irish case using a poverty line which combines information on income and life-style, we find that one in three of the poor come above the psychological distress threshold compared to one in eight of the non-poor.

The issue of the relative importance of unemployment and poverty must, to some extent, be an artificial one since unemployment is one of the major causes of poverty. The evidence, though, is clearly relevant to the issue of the relative significance of manifest and latent functions of employment. Jahoda (1981, 1982) argues that over and above the provision of financial rewards, employment serves a variety of latent functions by embedding the individual in a web of social relations. Our empirical analysis does indeed show that unemployment has a significant effect even among the non-poor, with those who are unemployed being five times more likely to come above the psychological threshold than those who are at work or retired. However, our results clearly indicate that the impact of unemployment is mediated, to a significant extent, by the fact that while less than one in fourteen of those at work or retired and non-poor exhibited mental health problems, the figure rose to well over four out of ten for those who suffer both poverty and unemployment.

REFERENCES

Eisenberg, P. and Lazerfeld, P. (1938) The Psychological Effects of Unemployment, *Psychological Bulletin*, 35: 358-90

Fox, A., Goldblatt, P. and Jones, D. (1985) 'Social Class Mortality Differentials: artefact, selection or life circumstances' in R. Wlikinson (ed) *Class and Health*, Tavistock, London.

Fryer, D. and Payne, R. (1986) 'Being Unemployed: a review of the literature on the psychological experience of unemployment' in Cooper, C. and Robertson, I. (eds) *International Review of Industrial and Organisational Psychology*

Fryer, D. (1992) 'Psychological or Material Deprivation ?' in McLaughlin, E (ed) *Understanding Unemployment: new perspectives on active labour market policies*, Routledge.

Goldberg, P. (1972) *On the Detection of Psychiatric Illness by Questionnaire*, Oxford University Press, London.

Kelvin, P. and Jarret, J. (1985) *Unemployment: its social psychological effects*, Cambridge University Press, Cambridge.

Moser, K., Fox, A. and Jones, D. (1984) 'Unemployment and Mortality in the OPCS Longitudinal Survey', *Lancet* 8, December: 1342-9.

Nolan, B. (1990) 'Social Economic Mortality Differentials in Ireland', *Economic and Social Review*, 21 (2):193-208.

Nolan, B. (1992) 'Poverty and Health Inequalities' in Callan, T. and Nolan, B. (eds) *Poverty and Policy in Ireland*, Gilland Macmillan, Dublin.

Warr, P. and Jackson, P. 'Men without Jobs: some correlates of age and length of unemployment', *Journal of Occupational Psychology*, 57(1): 77-86.

Wheaton, B. (1980) 'The Sociogenesis of Psychological Disorder: an attributional theory', *Journal of Health and Social Behaviour*.

1.4   Local Case Studies

1.4.1 Young People in West Belfast, Mr. Jim McCorry, EXTERN, Belfast

Extern set up a voluntary project in West Belfast, based on a model developed in England, to work with young people, engaged in deviant behaviour. With the best intentions but a very naive outlook, we set out to help in some way and in the process learned a lot from these young people.

We discovered two things. Firstly, these young people were not bad or evil. On the contrary, they were feeling, thinking, caring, hurting young people. Secondly, their "errant" behaviour (namely joyriding) was not the fundamental issue, but the symptom of a much deeper problem.

The project began with part-time work with cars for the young people. It developed to a stage where the workers and the young people became very close and indeed their lives became intertwined. Whilst the voluntary workers did not really know what they were doing, we realised that something different was needed, as beatings, imprisonments and shootings certainly had not worked. We looked for guidance from existing research and writing, but identified a large knowledge gap in our understanding of young people.

We therefore used a wide range of techniques (videos, tapes interviews, discussions with parents . . .) in an attempt to understand why young people begin and sustain a form of behaviour. We realised at this stage that the young people did not know, but certain other elements became clear.

The first was that a behaviour continuum exists and that the reason a person begins a pattern of behaviour is not necessarily the reason they continue it. With joyriding, the start is very much expressive, instrumental delinquency, whereas the reason to embark upon a criminal career may stem from economic and social factors. Take the 14 year old who progressed from stealing cars to hijacking cigarette lorries. With £3,000 in the bank, he had chosen a criminal career as the only good option. This continuum, therefore, explained some things but still did not answer the question – "Why?".

We went on to break behaviour down into two elements:

1. The time element: the young people pointed to boredom and trying to fill the time, as well as the relative ease in stealing a car.
2. Motivational factors: many factors were identified, the economic environment being the chief motivator. Other factors were social and commercial, such as advertising and the media, which create expectations in young people. These expectations are, for the most part, unattainable, but the influences and pressures are enormous.

Once again, our study was enlightening, but did not really yield the desired results and further analysis was undertaken. Behaviour was again broken down into two parts:

1. Psychological factors.
2. Sociological factors.

We looked at a spectrum of psychological factors, from childhood through to adulthood and identified those which may be indicators of errant behaviour, such as parental punishment, separation, parental stability, etc. We also examined the sociological side, for example, social disorganisation, culture and poverty machismo, material irregularities due to class differences and labelling theories.

The difficulty was that this did not provide much real information either. It identified an enormous range of reasons but provided no thread of commonality. It appeared that all the major theories neglected to identify any common thread in deviant behavioural patterns.

In my opinion, the real issue is the information, provided by society and its systems, which negates these young people as acceptable human beings. They cannot tie their objective reality to their subjective feelings because our culture is based upon the concept that if we do not work, we are nothing.

In order to counter this, it is necessary to identify and eliminate the source of the information and to create new information, showing these young people that they do matter.

The continuance of deviant behaviour may be illustrated in metaphor. The young person is the plant that strives and grows towards light. The young persons' light and that towards which he/she strives is, at some level, power. They engage in behaviours because of their perception of their power relationship with society. And it is this power perception which drives them on to sustain destructive behaviours.

This power is related to where we stand within the economic system. If the goal is to assert one's personal power, this will manifest itself in certain needs. If our young people are powerless and have no support systems in trying to achieve this objective, it is hardly surprising that they will persist in engaging in irrational behaviour. Not only will this behaviour continue but it will expand.

If we persist in demonizing the poor and unemployed and those who work on their behalf, it is we who shall create the underclass – the demons.

There are those, namely politicians, who argue that full employment is achievable. However, full employment cannot be achieved in any western nation, in any foreseeable future and the reasons are clear. Technology negates the need for it. Manufacturing multinationals have moved to where labour is cheaper. Finance capital has achieved a new importance. We cannot, therefore, continue to pursue policies built on full employment, because we are lying to our young people and not teaching them about the quality of life and life itself. Lastly, we have been told that we have to be neutral. I ask, how can anyone be neutral of the situation and at the same time fight as strongly as we can for the poor, impoverished and unemployed?

1.4.2 Craigavon – 'development' gone wrong, Dr. Carole Evans, Brownlow Health Centre, Craigavon

I am a G.P. involved in the running of Brownlow Health Centre in Craigavon. Brownlow was established as a new town in 1978. The plan was that eventually Brownlow would merge with Lurgan on the East and Portadown on the West and become a large new city called Craigavon. This never came to pass for a variety of reasons, including an unwillingness on the part of the Unionist parties to see through effective integration. Hence, Brownlow's health centre, built for 12 doctors, only has a staff of four and a half.

People have moved to Brownlow for many different reasons –
some came because of the availability of housing; others to escape
from troubled areas; and yet others in the hope of a fresh new start
to their lives. The town was built around a Goodyear plant, one of
the many multi-national corporations which moved into the country with promises of employment. It was established in 1976,
employing 1800 workers. When Goodyear pulled out, the effects
were evident in the large number of houses which came onto the
market. The government's decision to build a whole city around a
multinational was fundamentally flawed. Multinationals receive
huge grants, tax free incentives and are shown every possible way
to avoid paying tax, that the ordinary person in the street pays
every day of their life. When the grants and incentives begin to run
out, they begin to pare down the workforce and eventually pull
out. This is obvious in the case of Goodyear, who made seven to
eight hundred redundant in 1978, cut the workforce by another
700 in 1981 and by 1982 the plant was closed. Apparently they
relocated in Malaya, Singapore and in one other location.

The reasons fed to the press pointed to strikes, a militant
workforce etc,. However, the management at Goodyear stated that
they had never come across such a skilled, hard-working workforce.
This puts the lie to the idea that the workforce was militant and
that they were in financial trouble. Goodyear pulled out because
the grants had run out.

I think that the vast sums of money which are handed out to
multinationals should be re-channelled into our workforce and
skilled technicians and into creating lasting employment. We
should not be dependent upon the whims of foreign MNCs, who
will go where the grants take them.

Community workers, such as myself, act as "brooms" in cases
such as these. We are left to sweep up the parts and pieces of lives
that have been broken by the actions of the large multinationals
and the economic powers and try to pretend that a health service
exists. When Goodyear closed, our workload in the health centre
increased dramatically (though the number of doctors did not
increase proportionately). More women began to visit the health
centre with more complex problems (not always medical) and
men, who are traditionally less willing to visit the doctor, started to
turn to the health service. It became apparent, that especially in
the 30-plus age group, many of these men were displaying signs of
lack of hope, depression and an inability to know what to do. Here

were the signs of a community, devastated by the closure of the biggest employer and the lack of alternative employment. It had a disproportionate effect on the whole community. More women began to take up badly-paid, unskilled jobs, many of whom were at an age that they should not have had to engage in this type of work. Family life was turned upside down. The men now stayed at home, desperately seeking work and unwilling to admit how much the loss of their traditional role of wage-earner vexed them. Perhaps the 20% rise in male suicides in Britain may be an indicator of the reluctance of men to complain and express these feelings.

Christmas sees a peak in consultations. Patients attend with apparently minor medical problems, but after a while, their anxiety regarding finances and the family materialise. In Brownlow, whilst the official unemployment rate stands at approximately 30%, if the figures were divided along sectarian lines, this rate may well be up to 50 or 60%. A few examples may help to illustrate the current situation. One is the case of a young family. The husband was a skilled and able-bodied worker. The wife lost her job and six months later he too was out of work. His wife was pregnant and he tried desperately to find alternative employment but remained unemployed for seven years. His greatest joy became a few cans of beer at home on Friday nights. Thankfully, he recently found a job and is looking and feeling happier and healthier. However, for people such as in this family, consultation time at a local health centre is absolutely necessary in order to provide some small safety-valve during long-term unemployment.

Another example of the vital role played by health centres occurred when I was requested to certify a young woman. She had been beaten up by her husband just before they arrived for a consultation at the health centre. He wanted to have her certified. However, on consultation it emerged that they were living in a situation of intense poverty, with a handicapped child and were receiving no support. She had had no time off in six years and, one night, walked out of the house, leaving the child behind. As a result, he beat her. The role that the health and social services should have played in helping this family is vital.

In Northern Ireland, however, the new (since 1990) government contract for GPs seeks to cut down the number of general consultations, such as the general consultations I have provided for the young families in the examples above. GP's are now expected to run special clinics on diet, smoking, sex ... rather than use this valuable time to talk to patients and cater to their real needs. Currently, government economic and social policies are cutting into the poor and I believe that their health policies attempt to disguise this fact. Yet it is only through fundamental changes in economic and social policy, not the provision of 'lifestyle' clinics, that we shall see any improvements in health.

1.4.3 Unemployment in Tallaght, Michael Creedon and Brendan O'Donoghue, Tallaght Centre for the Unemployed

The development of Tallaght from a small village to one of three satellite towns of Dublin (the other two being Blanchardstown and Clondalkin) began in 1972. As the area grew, there was a marked lack of social, economic, environmental and cultural infrastructure to match this development. Tallaght was developed in an ad hoc manner, resulting in the lack of infrastructure and support services.

Tallaght, with a population of approximately 75,000 now, has an unemployment rate of 27%. Although this figure is very high, it does not relect the real problems facing this community. West Tallaght, with a population of over 17,000, the majority of whom are living in local authority housing, has an unemployment rate of over 46%. The Codan Report in 1987 indicated that the unemployment rate in this area was then over 46% and unemployment in Tallaght has risen since.

Tallaght has recently been granted a third level institution (Tallaght RTC) and a town centre (The Square), but still lacks some vital amenities, such as a hospital. And despite these new developments, unemployment continues to grow.

The Tallaght Centre for the Unemployed has a number of programmes which are aimed at dealing with the problem of unemployment. As the Centre develops, it is gaining a profile, within the areas with high levels of unemployment, as a caring organisation. As a result of this, more and more people are appearing at the Centre, hoping we can assist them overcome the problems associated with unemployment.

From our research project "Life on the Dole", three problems appear to dominate the day to day experiences of people who are long term unemployed. These are: a) boredom; b) financial hardship; c) the loss of psychological well-being. Exclusion from normal activities within the community is also a major problem indicated by this research.

In order to truly understand the problems of unemployment, it is perhaps essential to understand the benefits gained from employment. Unemployment is very often thought of in purely economic terms, ignoring the very real personal and social aspects of this problem. It also hides the needs of particular groups, who tend to be excluded from employment, including the disabled, handicapped and lone parents. It is, therefore, important to remember the personal and social aspects of unemployment, when attempting to deal with the problem.

Work is often perceived as employment but this is not necessarily true – for example, there is housework and voluntary work, neither of which are classed as employment. Employment is, however, perceived as the central part of a meaningful life. It is seen to provide income, status and identity. The unemployed are excluded from a say in many aspects of their lives, for example, the negotiations in relation to National Wage Agreements, such as the P.N.R./P.E.S.P. The terms of these agreements can affect people who are unemployed as much as those who are employed, so why are they excluded from having a direct input?

There is a very clear distinction between the employed and the unemployed. When a person loses a job, they lose the "integrity by which their self-image is maintained." There is no status left and they are perceived as having failed. They become socially isolated and the status of the "non-citizen" is realised. This is when psychological problems can develop.

Research has indicated a multitude of benefits to be gained from employment, and these are probably most clearly reflected in the most difficult aspects of unemployment identified above. From our research, involving a random sample interviewed at the local Labour Exchange, the following were the most common methods employed by the individual to deal with these difficulties:

* Hobbies
* Walking
* Positive Attitude

When asked what could be done to deal with the problems of unemployment, respondents replied:

* Increased Dole
* Absolutely Nothing

The overall findings of the research reinforce what the Centre has already discovered – that this is both an individual and a community problem. The Centre has not got the resources to deal with all of the people affected by unemployment. It is now necessary to develop means whereby other groups and agencies, with the ability to deal with this particular problem, may become interlinked.

We are only seeing the tip of the iceberg in relation to the overall problem, and the conclusion of our Centre to date is that more resources must be provided, otherwise these problems will become much worse and society as a whole will feel the consequences.

1.4.4 Connemara – the effects of emigration, Bridget Quirke, The Connemara Forum.

The Connemara Forum project is a model action project funded under the EC Poverty III programme (1990-1994). It is a rural development partnership of voluntary, community and statutory agencies based in North West Connemara.

The N.W. Connemara area is an area of c.300 square miles with a population of 8,608 (1986 Census). 1991 figures of 8,498 record a 1.3% population decline. Population density is amongst the lowest in Europe (9 persons per square kilometre as opposed to the European average of 51). The area includes the island of Inishbofin which experiences more acutely problems of distance and isolation, which are common throughout the area. N.W. Connemara as an identifiable community can be said to be a construct of Poverty III. However, it does coincide approximately with the boundaries of English-speaking Connemara. High levels of unemployment in North West Connemara (NWC) have had direct and indirect effects on population health status and on the provision of health care.

The direct effects of unemployment on health behaviour, morbidity and mortality are well documented. Adverse effects at all three levels of health status have usually been recorded in relation to rapid rises in unemployment, usually in the urban manufacturing sector, generally resulting from workforce reductions. While the consequences are likely to be less severe and more difficult to measure in rural, non-industrial settings, it is reasonable to assume that similar, though less pronounced, effects operate, particularly where baseline productivity is low.

Of greater importance are the indirect effects of unemployment mediated through selective outmigration from the young adults age band (18-30 years). Outmigration in this group has two major effects: (1) a distortion of normal epidemiological patterns in respect of disease and reproduction; and (2) alterations in the organisation and delivery of both formal and informal health care.

A reduction in numbers of the young adult age group results in a decrease in the denominator population with little reduction in disease burden. Young adults have low infections or degenerative disease rates and their removal from the population does not result in any major reduction in morbidity. At the same time their removal reduces denominator size resulting in a rise in incidence and prevalence rates for disease on a population basis. On the other hand, the fall in birth rates associated with selective outmigration will reduce the neo-natal component of morbidity/ mortality. Similarly accident rates, particularly motor and agricultural categories, will also decline. The effect of selective outmigration is to remove the most healthy component of the population and, by inference, leave the least healthy or more disease-prone section behind. Even within the migrant age group a fitness bias operates, whereby the less fit are less likely to migrate, making a further contribution to disease rates in the residual population. These migration effects result in increased general disease rates in a smaller population, with higher specific rates of chronic disease and lower rates of obstetrical hazards and accidents. As a result there is an increase in demand for services for the chronic diseases relative to the population base, with some residual, but declining, demand for maternity care (see figure 1).

Perhaps the most important effects of unemployment and related outmigration relate to the provision of health services, both formal and informal. In the formal sector, general depopulation, particularly in dispersed settlements such as those of NWC, makes it difficult to maintain statutory services at the periphery as economic efficiency arguments lead to progressive centralization. Unemployment and depopulation therefore have a secondary effect of reducing formal care at the periphery, often without the ability to replace it with informal or auxiliary services.

Figure 1:   Health Effects of Unemployment and Migration

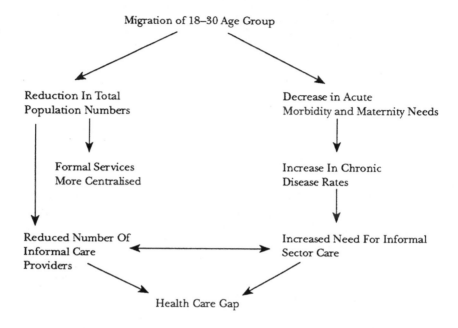

A related secondary effect of unemployment and selective migration on health care is the removal of voluntary labourpower from the informal system. This voluntary labourpower is particularly well suited to providing the health care required for chronic disease and geriatric needs, provided that it is adequately supported and remunerated. Thus, at a time when formal care systems are contracting, community labourpower resources are diminishing.

Thus unemployment leading to selective out-migration results in:

1. Increase in population morbidity/mortality rates arising from the removal of the low risk subgroups;
2. Reduction in formal services at the periphery (including maternity services) as population numbers and birth rates decline;
3. Increasing demand for informal and ancillary services as formal services.

In the absence of additional financing to the formal sector, these changes call for a re-structuring of the overall health care system and the development of new delivery systems and labourpower resources. The Connemara Forum's primary health project is directed at carrying out a review of these changes in health and disease patterns and the consequent changes in care needs under severe conditions of unemployment and outmigration. The Primary Health Project in N.W. Connemara is co-funded by the Western Health Board and the Forum. Its main aim is to develop the scope of the health care personnel and the community in the area, so they can become more actively involved in their own health care and, therefore, reduce their dependence on Galway-based tertiary services. This has so far involved:

a) Operations research on targeting and the scope and delivery of care in formal systems;
b) Epidemiology and service utilization studies for community intervention, planning and evaluation, conducted by members of the community;
c) Development of community-based care systems by training, education and technical support of voluntary care providers and their formal service counterparts;
d) Improvements and extension of the existing health information systems, to facilitate service co-ordination and delivery monitoring.

PART II:

RESPONSES TO THE

EFFECTS OF UNEMPLOYMENT

2.1   The Community Development Programme

Julia O'Neill, Principal Officer,
Voluntary, Community and Information Services, Dept. of Social
Welfare, Republic of Ireland

I would like to use this opportunity to outline briefly the Community Development programme, where the programme fits in to the role of the Department of Social Welfare and its links with other strategies to alleviate the effects of unemployment.

The Welfare Role of the Department of Social Welfare
The primary role of the Department of Social Welfare is income support. However, in recent years, there has been increasing emphasis in the Department on identifying ways of improving our clients welfare in the broadest sense and thereby improving the quality of their lives. The VCI Branch was set up in 1990 to manage all aspects of Social Welfare activities which have a welfare dimension. This includes:

> Voluntary and Community Services; The Community Development Programme; Grants for locally based women's groups; Grants for voluntary groups working in disadvantaged areas or with disadvantaged groups; Pilot projects to tackle the problems of managing on low income; Bursary schemes etc.; The Advice and Information Services of the Dept. of Social Welfare; The Supplementary Welfare Allowance scheme and the related welfare role of the Community Welfare Service.

The Community Development Programme
This programme, which was set up in 1990, provides financial assistance to locally-based projects in disadvantaged areas to assist with the staffing and equipping of local resource centres which provide a focal point for community development activities in the area. The projects encourage local voluntary and community

groups to develop partnerships with each other and link with statutory agencies in their area with a view to tackling the problems faced by the community. The programme is funded by the Department of Social Welfare and supported by the Combat Poverty Agency. The focus in the programme is on disadvantage and on giving resources to local communities to help them tackle their own situation and seek to improve it. To this end, we seek involvement of local people and members of "target" groups themselves in all aspects of the operation and management of the Projects.

Starting with 15, there are now a total of thirty projects in operation, or in the process of being set up, under the Community Development Programme this year. The establishment of these new projects represents a significant addition to the ability of the local community to respond to local social needs and to the range of services and opportunities available for the local people. Project areas are selected for inclusion in the Programme on a range of criteria including level of disadvantage and the existing base of community development activity in the area.

The Community Development projects are intended as mechanisms which will develop the local community infrastructure and will enable individuals and groups in the most disadvantaged communities to assert control over their lives, to participate in decisions that affect them and to be part of a process of change in their area. They have three main functions. These are:

* Practical Assistance: this ranges from providing advice and assistance to individuals and local groups (for example on welfare entitlements, local services, other groups in the area, on services and facilities, on funding opportunities) to the provision of practical services for local voluntary and community groups (for example, telephone, photocopying, printing facilities, library, meeting rooms etc.,).

* Development Work: this involves supporting and stimulating the work of local groups by acting as a catalyst for bringing groups together to identify needs, to identify how best these needs can be met, to draw up action plans and so on. They enhance the development process in their area – for example by organising training programmes for local projects, helping groups to acquire more skills and confidence, and organising personal development opportunities for local people.

* Partnership and Co-operation : community development
  resource centres provide a useful mechanism for building
  good relations between statutory bodies and community
  groups in an area and between community groups and a
  range of other interests in an area, for example, national
  voluntary organisations, the churches, local employers and
  trade unions.

The activities being undertaken or supported locally are only one
of a range of measures – Community Development Projects include projects with specific target groups such as the elderly,
young families, single parents, the unemployed as well as local
enterprise initiatives. In order to fulfil this support role,
community development resource centres receive core funding
(on average c.£50,000 pa) to employ professional staff and cover
basic running costs.

Community Development Resource Centres have been most
successful where there has been a very clear process for setting
them up with expert support, advice and training organised by the
Combat Poverty Agency. In these cases time has been spent in
developing effective management structures and clear and agreed
programmes of work. The Community Development projects have
benefited significantly from being part of a national programme
with all the resulting opportunities for learning from each others'
experience and from engaging in joint training initiatives.

**The potential for linkages between the Community Development
Projects and area-based enterprise/unemployment initiatives.**
Community Development initiatives of this type have the capacity
to be an important precursor of economic development and
hence employment in disadvantaged areas. The Community
Development Projects work with those who are most disadvantaged and excluded from the labour market in our society.

While separate from the PESP area-based response to long-term
unemployment and the new County Enterprise Partnership Boards
(see next section, 2.2), the Community Development Programme
is complimentary to these initiatives. The main difference
between them is that the Community Development Programme
concentrates on social and not just economic issues. Experience
has shown that the Community Development Programme serves
to enhance and strengthen the ability of the local community to

participate fully in the PESP initiative in areas where the two programmes overlap. This was recognised by the Government in setting up the County Enterprise Partnership Boards.

Discussions are now underway to ensure that effective linkages are developed between local Community Development Resource Centre projects and County Enterprise Partnerships, particularly their community development sub-committees. County Enterprise Partnerships have been set up specifically to address issues of enterprise creation, tourism, education and training support for the unemployed, especially the long-term unemployed, and related community development activity, although they will undoubtedly concern themselves with a broader range of local socio-economic issues.

Community Development Resource Centre projects have been established to support and encourage local community activity aimed at addressing all aspects of poverty and disadvantage. Thus, while sharing a concern about issues of employment creation, economic development and the needs of the unemployed, they are also concerned with the needs of the elderly, women and children, those with disabilities, the homeless, lone-parent families, young people at risk, travellers and other disadvantaged groups. Depending on the needs of an area, action can range from providing welfare information and advice to supporting playgroups, addressing issues such as housing, health, legal, transport and education services, promoting local arts and cultural initiatives and so on. Thus at times the work of local Community Development Resource Centres will relate to that of County Enterprise Partnerships and at times it will differ.

Concluding Remarks

The Community Development Programme has just reached the end of its first three years and is currently under review. It is hoped that the experience gained and lessons learned will enable us to develop an even more effective Programme in the future. The Department of Social Welfare is committed to the development and expansion of the Community Development Programme over the coming years and to building appropriate linkages with other initiatives to combat poverty and disadvantage.

2.2   The Contribution of Private-Public Partnerships to Local Development

Michael Priors, Dept. of an Taoiseach

The Programme for Economic and Social Progress (PESP) for 1991-1993, like its predecessor the Programme for National Recovery for 1998-1990, sets down government policy in Ireland in a comprehensive way for a three year period. Section VII of the PESP is titled the Area Based response to Long Term Unemployment. It sets down a new strategy to counter long term unemployment and the danger of it through action at the local level. The strategy is and will be area based, has and will have local communities as the primary movers, will integrate and involve a progression through various existing initiatives in the areas of enterprise development, job creation, education, training and community development.

Twelve Partnerships have been established to pilot the initiative, eight in urban and four in rural area. The Boards of the Partnerships (Figure 1) are representative of local communities, the social partners and the State and they have devised area action plans which address the specific needs and priorities of the area in terms of education, training and enterprise creation and community development with particular reference to services for the unemployed. These plans are strongly supported by the social partners at Central Review Committee level and at local level by the channelling of services and staff to assist in the implementation of the plans.

One possible model of an Area Action Plan is as shown in Figure 2. Such a plan would address in each catchment area the following issues:

* what resources are present – the people, skills, traditions, labour force (including people who are long-term unemployed, lone parents, disabled people, travellers and other

marginalised groups); industrial/commercial firms; natural resources and amenities?
* what are the area's development needs and opportunities in terms of education, training, employment enterprise and capacity building generally?
* what specific agreed programmes will be undertaken, by whom and within what time scale and how will the success of the action taken be measured?

Aside from facilitating various public bodies in providing integrated responses to particular initiatives, it is important to note that the employers have responded in a specific way by establishing the Enterprise Trust to undertake a national fund-raising drive for financing of enterprise initiatives primarily in the Partnership areas. These funds have a key role, together with Exchequer funds in providing matching resources for EC funding in the immediate and long-term.

Figure 1: Partnership Structure

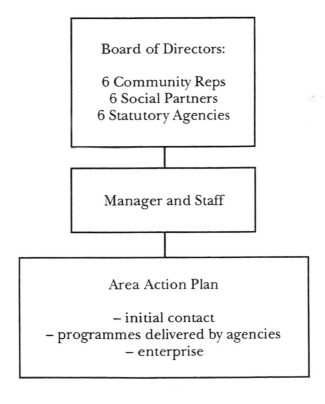

Figure 2: Area Action Plan

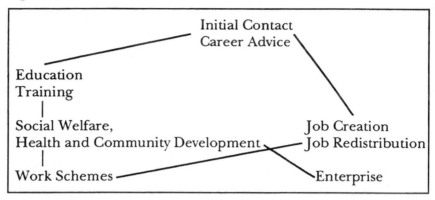

At national level a structure was put in place to bring the project into existence and to monitor and co-ordinate the activities of individual local companies (Figure 3). This was and is being undertaken by the Central Review Committee of the PESP representative of the social partners and Government officials. The Committee recommends appropriate arrangements to Government for decision with a high degree of certainty that its recommendations will be agreed upon.

Figure 3: The Central Review Committee

*   The Social Partners
*   Government
*   Chair – Secretary, Department of the Taoiseach
*   Permanent Secretariat

The Government in Sept./Oct. 1992 decided to extend the scope of the local development approach both geographically and in terms of content. This expanded locally based initiative will build on the work of the existing County Development Teams and of the Partnership companies put in place under the Programme for Economic and Social Progress in twelve areas through the county. It is in keeping with the PESP commitment to extend the area based approach nationwide.

Each county will have an Enterprise Company with a Partnership Board consisting of local community representatives, of business, trade union and farming representatives at the local county level and of the key public bodies, including local authority representation at both political and management levels. The County Enterprise Partnerships will provide a focus for and draw together the work of local community organisations in each county.

The County Enterprise Companies will have staff drawn from the local, regional and national development bodies. They will have specific enterprise, work and education objectives and will be funded through a combination of additional EC Structural Funding and Irish resources, both public and private. A special Jobs Fund in Small and Start-up businesses, in the order of £100 million, will be available to the Partnerships. The Partnerships will, in particular, act:

- to provide financial assistance for small and start-up businesses through a combination as required of grants, equity and interest subsidies;
- to provide training, education and other support in enterprise and business management skills, and especially marketing;
- to make available to people who wish to start their own businesses sound business ideas that will be drawn from the import lists by a small team drawn from An Bord Trachtala, the IDA and Eolas;
- to provide infrastructure and environmental measures relating or contributing to job creation, enterprise creation and business development, improving employability and other economic benefits for local communities.

The people in the team and others associated in piloting this approach are convinced that it provides a genuine opportunity for local effort and involvement in community regeneration. It is based on the view that such regeneration must be based on a comprehensive local economic consensus and social action plan at the local level and must be implemented by local partnerships. This is the underlying rationale which informs a number of approaches which are being put in place in Ireland at the moment to tackle both long-term unemployment and to promote local development generally. The objectives of this activity can be summarised as improving the skills, self-confidence and self-esteem of unemployed people, to change attitudes of employers, public servants and other key actors who are involved in the process of economic and social development and finally and most importantly to create more jobs. The PESP Partnership initiative is area-based, community-led, developmental, employment-focused and grant-aided and these considerations underpin the new County Enterprise Partnership approach.

2.3 Economic Development Strategies in Northern Ireland,

Mr. Perry McDonnell, Deputy Chief Executive, Training and Employment Agency

Introduction
The Training and Employment Agency is an economic development agency concentrating on the economic dimension.

The Nature of The Problem
Basically there is an excess of supply of people for available jobs. 67% of unemployed people find a new job within six months (and 75% of those within three months). But 50% of our unemployed people in Northern Ireland have – unhappily – qualified for long-term status.

Factors Influencing The Problem
Northern Ireland's current birthrate ensures that we will continue to have more people in the labour market than current rates of job creation can employ – the demographic tap is filling the workforce bathtub at least as quickly as competitive economic activity can empty it.

The greater pace of technological development and usage in industry requires more brain, less brawn.

We are trying to ascend a competitive escalator that is going in the opposite direction – we have to walk uphill to stand still and run to compete, and if that is not challenging enough our competitors are hell bent on quickening the pace.

Jumping off this escalator is not an option.

Economic Strategy In Northern Ireland And The Agency's Response
Our approach is to ensure that we are economically fit enough to stay on the escalator. The Northern Ireland economic development strategy is to develop competitiveness in people and

companies, leading to growth and, therefore, more jobs and less unemployment – dealing with the cause rather than the symptoms.

This means training and developing those already in, and those wanting to enter the workforce, in the skills which are needed in business and industry and which can be adapted to meet future demand. Our management development programmes, the Youth Training Programme, the Job Training Programme and the increased training element of our Action for Community Employment (ACE) Scheme are the major tools we use for developing the necessary abilities and qualifications in young people leaving education and for people who are unemployed. The percentage of people on schemes who subsequently get jobs is not as high as we would like it. But 36% of ACE workers last year did find jobs on leaving the scheme. This is a considerable improvement because ACE and those who provide the programme are getting better. On the YTP and JTP side, both are now being included in our new Job Skills concept and in the long-term this should improve the value and effectiveness of these schemes.

It also means enhancing companies' fitness to compete by helping them develop the skills of their existing employees – not least of which is the development of company managers. Our major programme directed at firms is our Company Development Programme.

The Scale of The Response
For young people there is a guarantee of training provision, and currently over 16,000 are benefiting from this through various strands of our Youth Training Programme.

There are almost 5,000 in training including in management training, and just under 10,000 in our ACE scheme. Training plans agreed within the Company Development Programme formally encompass a further 40,000 people.

Altogether, then, around 60,000 people in Northern Ireland are benefiting from some form of the Training and Employment Agency sponsored initiative aimed at improving both the economic prosperity of the individuals concerned and Northern Ireland as a whole.

Conclusion
There are no short-term employment initiatives which can be usefully sustained for any length of time unless the economy

grows and is strong enough to support them – our focus must therefore be on the longer term goals.

A strategy is necessary therefore which addresses some of the worst effects of unemployment in the short term, but is geared towards longer term economic growth in which more people can share the benefits.

2.4 The Trade Union Approach to the Needs of Unemployed People

2.4.1 Jack Nash, Regional Secretary, SIPTU

Unemployment affects both the unemployed and those in employment, who are currently wondering, "When is it going to happen to me? Over the last year I have been very much involved with the unemployed, those who find themselves out of a job. There is a need for a greater understanding of how the unemployed feel and the devastating effects of losing a job. Society is built upon the idea that to have a job means that you are a real person, a real contributor. On the other hand, if you do not have a job, you are of no use and are a drain on society's resources. In reality, it is people that matter. There are currently 14 million people unemployed in Europe and that figure is set to further increase by 500,000 over the next year. So, this must surely be everyone's problem.

The Sunday Tribune carried out a survey before the recent Irish general election and discovered that, out of those interviewed, 86% said that unemployment was their primary concern going into the election. It would also be a fair guess to say that the other 14% had unemployment down as their number two concern. This must surely reflect the real fears of everyone on the island with regard to unemployment.

Two situations brought home to me the seriousness of the problem. The first was the case of a 17 year old girl, who was a good worker with a clothing company, she was bright and hardworking, but could see no good reason to turn up for work every day. The union was called in and after hours of talking and probing, it transpired that she was the only person in her family and peer group who had to get up in the morning and go to work. Yet her family and friends seemed perfectly able to survive. Her lack of social skills and the influence of her home life and background meant that she could not see a reason to go to work every day. The important message here, is that it is necessary to fully understand the problem and its source, before ever attempting to find the solution.

The second instance was a highly successful company in Derry, with 450 well-paid, highly-skilled employees. One morning at 10.45am, the management announced that the factory was closing at 11.00am. The first reaction was desperation, the second an attempt to save the jobs and the community. Over a period of 147 days, 205 meetings took place, and through the efforts of the workforce and community the factory reopened with a staff of 150. This has since increased to the current 250 and the workforce is expected to continue to grow. The moral of the story is that, whilst we are all dependent upon the large economic power-holders, there is life after the multi-national.

The trade unions are responding in this way, and through the setting up of the Irish Trade Union Trust, are attempting to save companies in similar situations from closure. The trade unions have to handle unemployment on both a macro- and micro-economic level, as in my two examples above. As a result, we have identified a need for greater continuity in the transition from school-life to working-life. Young people have traditionally been told that hard-work at school is the necessary tool to gaining employment. However, many have discovered that this is not necessarily true, which points to failings in our education system. To counter this, employment schemes, such as the SES in the South and ACE in the North, have been instigated, but they, as far as the trade unions are concerned, are merely palliatives. However, criticism of these schemes has gone largely unheeded and they continue to be implemented. Young people are sent on training programmes, and are given hope for the future, in many cases they are abused and taken advantage of, and at the end of the day, there is nothing for them. We need to demand more. The situation has become a crisis of epidemic proportions and unless schemes are introduced that actually create jobs, be they in the public or private sector, there will be no useful result.

It is necessary to bring together the community and trade unions, in a spirit of co-operation, to solve the real problem of "loss of jobs". The effects of unemployment can be dealt with through unemployment centres and community groups, but "loss of jobs" is the issue that must be tackled. Recently in Derry a company advertised 140 jobs and 4,000 applications were received.

The majority of people in this country want to work and they should be allowed the opportunity to do so.

2.4.2 Mr. Peter Rigney, Industrial Officer, Irish Congress of Trade Unions (ICTU), with responsibility for Unemployment Centres in the Republic of Ireland

Since 1986, the ICTU has established a network of 26 Centres for the Unemployed throughout the country. This initiative was undertaken as a response to the huge increase in unemployment which took place in the early 1980's. Congress took the view that trade unions should take a broader view in representing unemployed people in addition to employed people.

In the Republic since 1987, wage bargaining has been centralised in the Programme for National Recovery (1987-1990) and the Programme for Economic and Social Progress (1990 -1993). In both of these programmes a significant emphasis has been placed on keeping the unemployment issue at the head of the political agenda. Yet a feature of the eighties was the removal of unemployment from the political agenda, with the slogan that "it was not up to the government to create jobs". There are varying views of the effectiveness of the centralised approach to wage bargaining. However, it is only by such a solidaristic view of wage bargaining that unemployment related issues can be placed on the National Economic Agenda.

Centres for the Unemployed have as their main focus the provision of services for unemployed people. The two main areas of service are social welfare and education. While social welfare advice addresses the short-term problems of coping, education provides one possible route out of unemployment. Studies have shown that unemployment and, in particular, long-term unemployment, are closely associated with a lower than average level of educational attainment. Unemployed Centres have been to the fore in providing daytime classes for the unemployed.

They have also been to the fore in pushing for a broader range of schemes in the education sector which would be attractive to unemployed people. One particular example of this is the vocational training opportunity scheme, which from modest beginnings now provides approximately 2,000 places for long-term unemployed people to pursue studies towards a certificate.

It must be recognised that unemployed people are not a homogeneous group. To the extent that resources must be prioritised,

ICTU takes the view that they should be channelled towards the long-term unemployed – that is, those out of work for more than twelve months.

The question of unemployment will be around for some time to come. While it will come to the fore at election time, we must ensure that it stays top of the agenda, and that concern about the issue is not deflected by concepts such as the so-called leisure society or the traditional free market approach that jobs will be provided solely by the operation of the market.

2.5 Disability Action (NI)

Monica Wilson, Director, Disability Action, Northern Ireland.

At present, there are 201,000 adults with disabilities in Northern Ireland, which represents 17.4% of the population. One in four people is affected by disability issues and disabled people are up to five times more likely to be unemployed than non-disabled people.

Legislation relating to employment and disability is governed by the *Disabled Persons Employment Act* of 1944. This legislation has long been out-dated and it's shortcomings point to the need for legislative support in reforming this area of employment law.

Economic and social policy has long been designed to segregate disabled people from the community. "Special" schools and facilities have been set up, although the term "special" has not been defined. One thing that is clear from the treatment of disabled people is that it does not mean "better" and, in many cases, it does not even mean "equal". Disability is often equated with 'sufferers', 'victims' and 'handicap'. The term 'handicapped' originates from the concept of "cap in hand" and is a reinforcement of the negative stereotyping of disabled people. With regard to employment, definitions of disability should be vocational – that is, definitions should relate to the functions of jobs. This does become complicated, but it is necessary to move away from the medical sphere into an economic and vocational sphere.

With regard to employment policy, under the *Disabled Persons Employment Act*, a quota system is currently in place in Northern Ireland. In the private sector, 3% of the staff of a company with 20 employees or more, should be people with disabilities, recruited from a voluntary register of disabled people, held by the Training and Employment Agency.

The vast majority of companies do not comply with this system. Since the '70s, a mere 10 prosecutions have taken place in Britain. Of these 10 prosecutions only seven companies were found guilty and fines totalled £334. This indicates a lack of official support for enforcement. We have reached a situation where "persuasion and patronage" are the order of the day in the policy approach to disability and employment.

The disadvantages faced by disabled people are systemic and result from wrong attitudes and perceptions. People with disabilities are seen as passive, dependant, unable and ill. Disability is located in a medical context. It is Disability Action's aim to move the disability debate to a more appropriate social context. The issue is equal treatment, not different treatment, and the need for equal treatment can be seen in the lower wages earned by, and the few opportunities for career development for, disabled people. Even many voluntary organisations do not provide physical access for disabled people or access to information in formats suited to deaf people, people with learning disabilities, on tape or in large print.

It is essential, therefore, to empower people with disabilities, to provide support services in order to achieve a level playing field and to resource user projects rather than traditional models. Disabled people have the same need and desire to work and achieve as non-disabled people. In order to fulfil these objectives, schemes need to be put in place. It is necessary for people with disabilities to be able to access networks and to be encouraged to join them. Awareness training for both disabled and non-disabled people is required to eliminate negative stereotyping and to empower us. Disability Action provides a range of services, including an employment service, to enable networking. We provide guidelines for employers, providing information which will enable them to move away from discriminatory practices.

Disability Action operates, in partnership with the Training and Employment Agency, four main employment and training services: the Sheltered Placement Scheme; the Youth Training Programme Support Service; Employment Officers; and the Job Training Programme Support Service. The Sheltered Placement Scheme began in 1988 when Disability Action was invited by the Training and Employment Agency to establish a sponsorship which would ensure a high quality of service and which would promote the integration of disabled employees into the workplace. Special consideration was also given to the needs of employees with severe learning disabilities. The aim is to help people with disabilities achieve the right to work and to reach their full potential in employment. High quality support facilitates thus aim for service users and the funding agency. By March 1993 there were 118 employees employed by Disability Action under the Sheltered Placement Scheme. By far the biggest group is employees with a physical disability (42%). The next largest single group is those with some severe learning disability (19%), although a proportion of employees in other groupsings have some degree of learning disability. Sensorily impaired employees account for 13% of the total and in general this group is the most likely to transfer to open employment. To date, 13 employees have transferred to open employment. Such transfer will continue to be the aim for a proportion of employees but the Scheme is targetted at people with disabilities who may never move to open employment. In addition some of those transferred to open employment as the result of high productivity have already demonstrated a continued need for support which has or may in the future affect the security of their placements.

The Youth Training Programme Support Service caters for those individuals who have a physical disability and who wish to enter mainstream Youth Training. The Service aims to raise awareness of the needs of trainees with disabilities and to empower them to speak for themselves. It assists trainees to identify their needs in relation to training such as appropriate skills development, personal effectiveness, physical access, work placement, health and safety. The type of support provided could be equipment-based so that the trainee could then learn vocational skills. Alternatively support could take the form of negotiating with the trainee an appropriate action plan for personal development such as a self management programme, for example in independent travel or personal care. The Support Worker often acts as a co-ordinator between family members, social workers, occupational therapists, careers officers, work experience providers and the Training Organisation. The Support Worker acts as an advocate where the aim is to ensure the young person is provided with an equal opportunity to the training facilities offered by the Training Organisation. The support role carries an underlying responsibility to overview the effectiveness of training based on the trainees expectations and competence. The Support Worker works with the Careers Service of the Training and Employment Agency from where all referrals to the Service originate. The range of individuals using the Service are primarily those with multiple disability including learning difficulties and hidden disability. Numbers of young people opting for mainstream training have steadily increased over the least few years. Of the 115 individuals referred to the Service to date, around 40 are provided with direct support each month.

Disability Action has three Employment Officers based in Belfast, Craigavon and Derry, who provide a support service to employers, disabled people and others interested in promoting equality of opportunity for disabled people. Employer queries included requests for information on recruitment and selection procedures, advice on how to conduct disability surveys among existing staff, requests for comments on draft equality documents, and networking employers with the Disablement Advisory Service and with the relevant Disablement Employment Advisor. Work with employers has also included support for a number of Business in the Community Seminars. The range of enquiries from disabled people themselves include such issues as job security, employment-related benefit entitlement, opportunities for training, employment rights, registration with the Training and Employment Agency and networking with a number of organisations. Each of the Employment Officers has regular contact with local day centres and Disability Awareness Training in relation to employemnt issues has been delivered to day centre staff on a number of occasions. The Officers also worked with centre users and their key workers. The Employment Officers have also developed closer links with Colleges of Further Education during 1992. In two colleges, the North-West Institute of Further & Higher Education and Banbridge College, Employment Officers have been involved in implementing courses designed particularly for disabled people.

The Job Training Programme Support Service is a pilot programme operating in the Belfast area, offering support and assistance to disabled people, training organisations and placement providers participating in the Job Training Programme. The Support Service was developed to: assist those with disabilities seeking to join the Job Training Programme by providing information on the programme and how to gain access to it; support individuals during the duration of their programmes; assist Managing Agent staff in compiling suitable training programmes and in seeking appropriate placement providers for their disabled JTP participants; support placement providers by offering advice and assistance where necessary. By early 1993, 163 disabled people had used the Service, and of that number, 23% have come from day care, reinforcing Disability Action's belief that many people in day care are inappropriately placed and are capable of economic activity – something which is true for far more disabled people of working-age than either government, employers or the general population have yet grasped.

Society must recognise the disadvantage faced by people with disabilities and move to offset it, so that disabled people attain equal rights as citizens in Northern Ireland. None of this, however, can be achieved without official support, in terms of enforceable legislation. At the moment, in effect, disabled people do not appear to be included in employment policy and we are examining this, with a view to campaigning strategies for change. Most importantly of all disabled people should no longer be willing to take the blame for being unemployed and disabled.

2.6 Healthy Public Policy: guidelines for action

Brendan Dineen and Cecily Kelleher, Dept. of Health Promotion, University College Galway

As Nolan and Whelan have shown (section 1.3), observational data strongly supports an association between unemployment and ill-health. It can be difficult to separate the effects of unemployment per se from other indicators of socio-economic deprivation. For obvious reasons, unemployment is particularly associated with lower income groups. The latter in itself is associated with relatively poor health. However, there are undoubted psychological ill-effects related to chronic unemployment, manifesting themselves as depression, low self-esteem and secondary dependency. There are differences in responses by men, women and different age-groups, as might be expected. For practical purposes, the impact of unemployment is just one further example of the impact of inequity on health and well being. It is of the utmost importance that the health, as well as the social ill-effects, of unemployment be stressed. It is also necessary to both enable opportunities and provide choice for the unemployed.

Health promotion is a process by which individuals can take control of their own health. Landmark elements of this include the Who Targets for the Year 2000 and the Ottawa Charter (see Figure 1). This Charter stressed the importance of:

a) healthy public policy; through b) the strengthening of community action and participation; c) the creation of supportive environments; d) the development of personal and inter-personal skills; and e) reorientating and balancing hospital and community-based services.

By any criteria, unemployment is health-demoting. In order to tackle the problem, unemployment must be seen as a policy matter for health planners. Even the sceptical certainly recognise that increased health service utilisation is a consequence of unemployment. There are copious data on health-related behaviour, including increased doctor consultation rates, hospital referral, sick leave and disability pension. This represents a further incentive both for prevention of the problem and more appropriate management after its occurrence. In terms of health planning, it is insufficient to adopt a health education approach. Health education involves some form of communication designed to improve knowledge and develop understanding and skills which are conducive to health. In contrast, health promotion is not only concerned with enabling the development of lifeskills and individual competence to influence factors determining health, but is also concerned with environmental intervention to reinforce factors supporting healthy lifestyles. Thus, healthy public policy is concerned with three principal areas: specific groups of people (youth, women, elderly); services (work, equity, care); and products (education, drugs and food). The cornerstones of healthy public policy are an understanding of the interrelationships between the environment, economic status, personal choice, the health of the individual and of the society, and wideranging preventative health strategies, involving health promotion, health education, community participation and inter-sectoral planning. Thus healthy public policy is holistic and ecological, involving an integrated view of people's physical, mental and social dimensions. It is based on shared responsibility for health between governments, community and individuals and is not based on 'victim blaming'.

Figure 2 shows the current core structure for health promotion in the Republic of Ireland. The Republic of Ireland has an intersectoral Cabinet sub-committee on health promotion, chaired by the Minister for Health. An important aspect of their work deals with nutritional health promotion, especially for low-income families. This sub-committee represents one important forum for policy discussion, which is currently under-utilised. The National Advisory Council on Health Promotion recognises equity as a key feature of good health and, so also represents a forum for further examination of this issue.

Figure 1

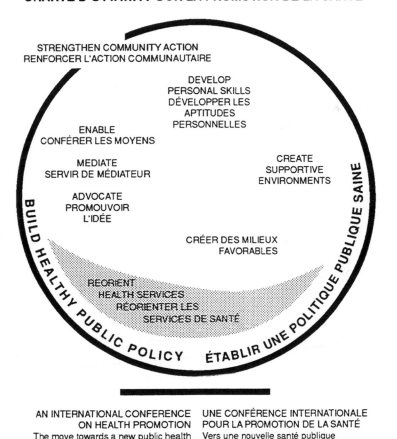

OTTAWA CHARTER FOR HEALTH PROMOTION
CHARTE D'OTTAWA POUR LA PROMOTION DE LA SANTÉ

Figure 2: Health Promotion in Ireland – the core structure

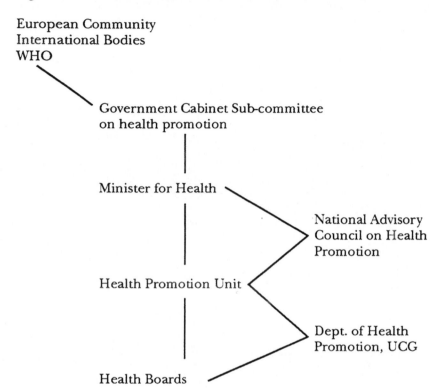

2.7 Statutory responses to health and social care needs in the context of high unemployment:

DHSS (NI), Western Health and Social Services Board (NI), North Eastern Health Board (Rep. of Ireland)

2.7.1 J.J.M. Harbison, DHSS (NI)

Northern Ireland has a population which experiences high levels of deprivation and unemployment, and the strategy adopted by the Dept of Health and Social Services (DHSS) must reflect the health and social care needs experienced in this population. The recent emphasis on the maximisation of health gain as distinct from concentration on extending services has further influenced the direction and nature of policy development.

The importance of such influences on Northern Ireland's policy for promoting health and social well-being is documented in the current Regional Strategy for the Health and Personal Social Services for the period 1992-97. This paper (published in late 1991) underpins the developments and priorities for the Health and Social Services for the next five years. The key characteristics of the strategy are a recognition that promoting the health and social well-being of the population necessitates the participation of many groups and organisations in the community to support the key role of the Health and Social Services themselves. These other players range from individual members of the population who must, for example, modify their lifestyles to reduce their risk of ill-health or social problems, to government agencies in the fields of education, housing and environment, who have a key contribution to make to overall health and wellbeing through the adoption of appropriate policies and action.

The Strategy is based on four key themes, two of which are of particular relevance in responding to the special needs of the disadvantaged. The first, the development of action on health promotion, has as its particular challenge the encouragement and support of people and structures to adopt a healthier way of life and to assist in obtaining both the information and skills necessary to improve health. The second theme covers the targeting health and social needs; accumulating evidence exists as to the extent of inequalities in the health and social well-being of the population, and the strategy directs Boards to initiate action in response to these inequalities.

The type of response likely to be effective in reacting to such special needs are considered. Of particular importance here is the requirement for the Health and Social Services Boards to assess the health and social care needs of their resident population and develop their purchasing decisions accordingly. Other possible approaches include the geographical targeting of areas where special attention is required, developing the role of general practitioners in identifying and responding to local need and initiating inter-Agency working arrangements with key other bodies whose work impacts on health and social needs.

The strategy also identifies a requirement for Boards to develop the participation of their population in the decision-making process about health and social care needs as well as participating in decisions as to the most appropriate manner in which these needs are considered. The potential for a community development based approach to facilitate such participation will also be encouraged.

2.7.2 Dominic Burke, Director of Social Care, Western Health and Social Services Board (NI).

Health and Social Services Boards in Northern Ireland exist to provide appropriate services for the assessed needs of their resident population. To deliver this agenda each Board is responsible for:

a) Assessing need;
b) Purchasing services;
c) Contracting for those services;
d) Monitoring the services.

The main emphasis in assessing needs and developing services is on a Programme of Care basis, including targeting specific groups, such as children, the disabled, etc. The aim is also to develop community services and where possible to enable these services to be received in the home or near/similar to a home environment as can be achieved. On this basis, the plan is to set about a series of

Figure 1: Social Care

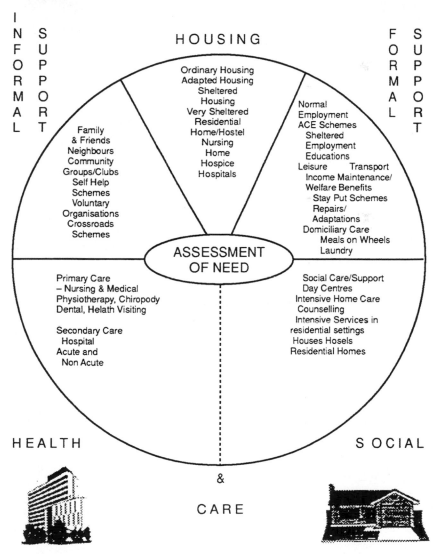

SOCIAL CARE

INFORMAL SUPPORT

FORMAL SUPPORT

HOUSING

Ordinary Housing
Adapted Housing
Sheltered
Housing
Very Sheltered
Residential
Home/Hostel
Nursing
Home
Hospice
Hospitals

Normal
Employment
ACE Schemes
Sheltered
Employment
Educations
Leisure   Transport
Income Maintenance/
Welfare Benefits
Stay Put Schemes
Repairs/
Adaptations
Domiciliary Care
Meals on Wheels
Laundry

Family
& Friends
Neighbours
Community
Groups/Clubs
Self Help
Schemes
Voluntary
Organisations
Crossroads
Schemes

ASSESSMENT
OF NEED

Primary Care
– Nursing & Medical
Physiotherapy, Chiropody
Dental, Helath Visiting

Secondary Care
Hospital
Acute and
Non Acute

Social Care/Support
Day Centres
Intensive Home Care
Counselling
Intensive Services in
residential settings
Houses Hosels
Residential Homes

HEALTH

SOCIAL

&

CARE

programmes, to enable the providers of health and social services to relate to the people and their needs, as well as the needs of their carers. The services should be creative and innovative and cater towards individual needs.

The Programme of Care began through the publication of the Social Care Review, to establish the quality and quantity of current services. This was circulated widely in order to gain a clear picture. This is now to become a yearly report. Focus groups were set up to achieve more targeted consultation. The focus group involving disabled people, for example, yielded a video entitled "Nobody ever asked me", about the statutory services not consulting with those for whom their services are being provided.

Northern Ireland Needs Assessment (NINA) is an attempt to collect all available information which focuses on peoples needs. It has involved bringing in specialist groups, in order to identify the needs of particular groups. Furthermore, information packs for the different areas have been produced.

To take an example of the types of programmes being introduced, it is worthwhile examining the Foyle Community Research Project, a pilot project being run on a housing estate, which aims to assess current services and needs. Figure 1 is the type of model being implemented in this programme. But in order for a programme like this to be any way successful, it is essential that the people who are affected have an input. It would be fruitless for the statutory agencies to work in isolation.

2.7.3 F. Howell, Specialist in Public Health Medicine, Director of Community Care and Medical Officer of Health, North Eastern Health Board (Rep. of Ireland).

The North Eastern Health Board is responsible for the delivery of health care, in association with other state funded bodies, in the counties of Louth, Meath, Monaghan and Cavan. These services are provided free of charge to approximately 39% of the population. Eligibility for provision of free services is based on means-testing. The remainder of the population are obliged to pay for some of the services.

Unemployment in the region is a significant problem with the overall number of unemployed people standing at 21,482 or 13% of the 15-64 population, and within the area there is quite a wide range of unemployment rates – for example, Meath 7%, Louth 19%. However, the debate as to the health consequences of this unemployment has not really been addressed in this country. Very little research into this area has been carried out as morbidity and mortality data are very crude and do not facilitate a proper analysis to be carried out using unemployment as a variable.

Whilst unemployment itself is not directly targeted, it is targeted indirectly by using income as a proxy measure. The North Eastern Health Board assesses eligibility on income grounds – if an individual or family's income falls below a specific level (for example, £79.50 a week for a single person living alone up to 65 years of age), with an adjustment to take account of expenditure on rent and medicines, then free access to medical services is available for them. Further, the Health Boards, through their Community Welfare Officers, also administer a Supplementary Welfare Allowance Scheme, a Free Fuel Scheme, Exceptional Needs Payments and a contribution towards burial (!) if required. They also act as an information source which directs a client to other agencies where they may have entitlements and who may be able to assist them.

As yet, the Health Authorities do not have a specific proactive preventative role in the area of the health consequences of unemployment although they are continuously aware of this problem. It is hoped, with the establishment of Departments of Public Health Medicine within each Health Board, that this whole area can be addressed.